The Catholic Case for Trump

The Catholic Case for Trump

Austin Ruse

REGNERY
PUBLISHING
A Division of Salem Media Group

Regnery® is a registered trademark of Salem Communications Holding Corporation

ISBN: 978-1-68451-096-2
eISBN: 978-1-68451-097-9
Library of Congress Control Number: 2020932588

Published in the United States by
Regnery Publishing
A Division of Salem Media Group
300 New Jersey Ave NW
Washington, DC 20001
www.Regnery.com

Manufactured in the United States of America

10 9 8 7 6 5 4 3 2 1

Books are available in quantity for promotional or premium use. For information on discounts and terms, please visit our website: www.Regnery.com.

*To my mother Dorothy Thompson and
my step-father Richard Thompson,
original Trumpers*

CONTENTS

Introduction

M illions of Americans are rallying around our polarizing president. Trump voters from 2016 are itching to cast their ballots again. If you have any doubt of that, just look at his massive rallies and record primary vote tallies. And while few have ever doubted the loyalty of Trump's base, the president has also won over scores of Republicans who held their noses and reluctantly voted for him in 2016. Those who were begrudging Trump voters are now enthusiastic Trump boosters. Even the Republicans who could not stomach casting a ballot for Trump and voted third party are now in Trump's column. They might say, "I could not vote for such a vulgar huckster with a shady past, but, you know, he has done a good job and, I hate to say this, he has actually grown on me." Of course, Democrats and hard-core NeverTrumpers are still virulently anti-Trump. They will never be convinced.

Lots of Americans are puzzled by Trump, but much of his political success can be explained by a simple fact: Americans are sick of the condescending, so-called experts inserting themselves into their lives.

President Trump has brought a heavy dose of common sense to our expert-ridden politics. That's why he drives many of his advisers nuts, who as "experts" themselves are often detached from commonsense decision-making. It also explains why his supporters love him so passionately. The experts, all of them—in the government, the law, the judiciary, the academy, and the media especially—tend to think they are better than the common citizen. Whenever "the experts" reach a conclusion that is deeply unpopular among the American people, they sneer and write off the people's objections as a product of ignorance.

And as if that weren't enough, they think they know better than their boss, President Trump. He knows it. We know it. But Trump does not care about their jeers and will not abandon common sense by deferring to experts who have discredited themselves time and time again. Whether they are three-star generals, partners at white-shoe law firms, or guys with decades of senior government service, they have one job: to give the elected boss their advice but never to get too high and mighty.

In recent years, we Catholics have seen our faith become the target of expert opinion. Experts now believe that it is their duty to expunge traditional practitioners of the Catholic faith. We are just as much the enemy as Donald Trump as the endless lawsuits against individual Catholics and Catholic organizations make clear.

The experts want to socially engineer a post-Christian society, and we are in their way.

Donald Trump is the man bringing the march of "expert" opinion to a halt. He stands for ordinary Americans, common sense, and traditions. He is the last bulwark against a radical Left that wants to destroy our way of life by any means necessary. But don't just take my word for it. In these pages, we'll cover the most important reasons why President Trump is a blessing to American Catholics. We'll take on the arguments of the Catholic Left and show precisely why four more years of the Trump presidency is necessary for serious Catholics. In short, we'll make the Catholic case for Trump.

CHAPTER 1

Trump the Man

Donald Trump is an acquired taste. He is not for everyone, and no one can be talked into him. While some took to Trump right away, others resisted and then came around later. Many will never support Trump, no matter how convincing an argument you present to them. Trump is a journey you take alone.

For a politician, Trump's character is uniquely polarizing. We're used to sweet-talking, suave politicos who twist themselves in knots in their efforts to win over voters. Trump is certainly not of that variety. He is a larger-than-life personality whose manner and style often loom larger than his policy agenda. Some voters love that personality, while others hate it. So, while any voter, and especially Catholic voters, can appreciate Trump's policy accomplishments, his perceived character is often a sticking point. That's why it's essential to start with Trump the man before addressing his considerable policy accomplishments.

Trump voters—whether Catholic or not—have already dealt with the more flawed aspects of his life story. Those who were reluctant to vote for him because of those imperfections now have nearly four years of his accomplishments that may help them overcome that reluctance. But despite his flaws, which we will address in due course, Trump's character has considerable virtues.

Donald Trump is a different kind of politician, and that has served him well in the current political climate. American politics is as divided today as ever. Partisan polarization did not start with Trump; it didn't even start with Obama. An argument can be made that the great polarization began as far back as 1987, when Senators Teddy Kennedy and Joe Biden borked Judge Robert H. Bork before the Senate Judiciary Committee. Conservative voters certainly remember how genteel Republican leadership barely fought back against the slander and invective Democrats launched at Judge Bork. Most elected Republicans considered it ungentlemanly to fight back, not realizing that the attacks against Bork were an attack against their constituents.

After the success of the Bork smear campaign, Democrats started to play by a new set of rules. By weaponizing the media, they tried to pressure their colleagues across the aisle into submission. Republican officials didn't get the memo, but conservative citizens saw the new state of play. Conservatives remember how the Democrats tried to lynch Clarence Thomas. We remember how the Left burned George W. Bush in effigy, calling him a fascist and Hitler, while he remained "presidential" and above the fray. Some may have been proud of him for taking the high road, but many wished he would fight back. That was all the more true when Democrats used the same playbook against the gentleman Mitt Romney, who likewise responded by refusing to defend himself. When they accused him of giving people cancer and of pushing granny in a wheelchair off a cliff, he said nothing.

After nearly three decades of lost political battles, a rather plainspoken, gruff, and often hilarious non-politician came along who knew the enemy, never gave an inch, and always gave back ten times more than he got. As Lincoln said about Grant, here was a man who fights. And in most glaring contrast to previous Republicans, Donald Trump recognized that the press, the Democrats, and the elites in his own party were often willing to work together to oppose conservative causes. He knew from the beginning that he was in a three-front war that previous "gentleman presidents" and candidates had refused to acknowledge.

Did Trump sometimes fight in ungentlemanly ways? Sure. Did he call names? All the time. Did he call names too much? Maybe, but the fact that he fought back was more important than the way he did it. God Almighty, his fans love that he fights. Sure, sometimes he shoots himself in the foot, but fighting back against slander meant that he stood up for conservatives whom establishment politicians repeatedly threw under the bus.

By the time Trump showed up, conservative Republicans were convinced that we lived under different rules than everyone else. While some sob sisters on the Right try to enforce this different set of rules, most conservatives are focused on achieving policy victories. As professional conservatives worried about decorum and appeasing leftists, Trump joked about how his supporters would stand with him even if he shot someone on Fifth Avenue.

In his masterful *The Case for Trump*, the great Victor Davis Hanson compares Trump to a fictional character in the movie *High Noon*, Shane, a mysterious gunfighter who is hired by a settler as a farmhand and then called upon to save the town from a ruthless cattle baron. Pushed to the limit, Shane is forced to gun down three of the cattle baron's men, delivering the town from the cattle baron's clutches. Thanks to Shane's heroism, the town can develop into a respectable place. But for that very reason, Shane himself is no longer welcome. Shane is a barbarian, and there is no room for a man like him in this civilizing place.

Hanson argues that someone like Trump is destined to do his job only to be rejected by the people he saved, to die in ignominy, never to be invited to those chummy group photos with previous presidents, the ones that grate on us so much: photos of George Bush grinning ear to ear with Bill Clinton, whom he now calls a "brother from another mother"; grinning even with Barack Obama and his wife Michelle, both of whom hold us in utter contempt. Trump will never be accepted by the elite cabal. But he will be remembered by those of us whom Obama called "bitter clingers" and Hillary called "deplorables." We are Joey shouting, "Come back, Shane."

■　　■　　■

New York City is a big place, where every neighborhood and borough is filled with different characters. To understand how a big-talking New York real estate mogul was able to win over conservatives across the country, you have to know a little bit of New York geography.

Donald Trump made his name in Manhattan, but he had to take a bridge or tunnel to get there. He was born in Queens, making him a "bridge-and-tunnel" person, as the Manhattan upper crust dismissively refer to people from the outer boroughs. Today, the outer boroughs are populated by trendy hipsters and millennials, but when Trump came up, high society viewed bridge-and-tunnel folk as crude and uncouth. They made fun of their accent, likening their "deez" and "doze" to cartoon mobsters.

Trump's dad started building single family homes and apartment buildings in Queens. Aside from Staten Island, Manhattan elites held Queens in the lowest regard. Brooklyn had a kind of mythos, as did the Bronx. But Queens? That was a backwater that might as well be flyover country for all the cosmopolitans cared.

That's where Trump came from, and he had big plans to conquer Manhattan even if he had to take a tunnel or a bridge to get there. He brought his accent with him (interesting that he appears never to have tried to lose it). And he brought along a chip on his shoulder, a feeling he was better than the white-shoe fops of Manhattan who couldn't help but look down on him.

The late Governor Mario Cuomo had a similar experience. Cuomo attended a Catholic law school in Queens, but when he crossed into Manhattan, the upper-crust law firms refused to give him a second look. Rumor has it he applied for jobs at fifty of them and never got a nibble. Cuomo wasn't just a Catholic, he was a wop, a dago. The WASPs who went to tonier schools looked down on Cuomo in the same way they looked down on Trump. When Cuomo landed at a small Brooklyn law firm, he would go on to represent Trump's dad, Fred.

Trump grew up on construction sites with rough men who spoke Queens English, not *the* Queen's English. They didn't have genteel manners and, in typical New Yorker fashion, didn't hesitate to speak their minds. As it turns out, bridge-and-tunnel people had a lot in common with working Americans across the country. That's why Trump resonates so well with working men and women, even though he's always wearing a suit and tie. He does not pander to them by wearing jeans and plaid shirts like a Romney would have done. He understands them because he knows them. They know him, too. They recognize him. In a very clear way, he is one of their own, even though he is a boss.

So many aspects of Trump's character can be traced to the Queens in which he grew up and the cutthroat world of New York real estate that he made his name in.

Consider Trump's skepticism of "expert advice," which has aggravated journalists and Washington insiders to no end. In the real estate world, if you give bad advice, you better not expect people to take you seriously the next time you chip in. Making mistakes has consequences in the real world, and the people whom Trump trusted for advice were expected to deliver results. Trump promised to do the same thing in our nation's capital.

Washington experts aren't used to being judged by the fruits of their labor. Instead of being held responsible for their actions, politicians and bureaucrats often fail up the organizational chart to leadership roles. Donald Trump was elected to end the failed policies of the political establishment. And yet, even after Trump's resounding win, the establishment kept carting out "experts" to defend those policies. Remember the famous "Tank Meeting," where a gaggle of policy elites ambushed Trump in a secure Pentagon room to teach him how the world works? Imagine the hubris it takes to talk down to the duly elected president of the United States. Trump was furious and let them know.

From the point of view of a real estate mogul, everyone is a vendor. Trump brought that attitude to politics. For Trump, the various experts are simply vendors offering him a product. As the lead on his governing project, he is free to "purchase" their advice if he thinks it's sound, but he's also free to walk away if he thinks they're offering him a bad deal. It doesn't matter whether they are selling foreign policy advice, legal advice, or political advice; none of them better lord their special knowledge over him. He is responsible for considering all of the domains together when he makes a decision. When a vendor pretends that he knows better than the client, the client has every right to get angry.

Trump's eagerness to take people to court is also a product of his Queens real estate background. Trump is widely criticized for what many see as his litigious nature. He has been sued multiple time. He has sued and often threatens to sue his adversaries. But in real estate, suing vendors is par for the course. Litigation is a fact of the building trades. Builders sue vendors, and vendors sue builders. A longtime Queens born and bred banker explains it this way: "There's a crack in this foundation, you need to reduce your invoice by 50 percent or I'll sue." Now, was there a crack? Was it big enough for a 50 percent reduction in price? Maybe, maybe not. But you might get something knocked off the price by negotiating with a threat. And don't forget, there's a good chance the other guy padded his invoice because he knew it was going to be renegotiated. And he probably knew you knew it. It's a tough business. That's just the way it is.

But right away, this puts Trump at odds with our idealized vision of how business should be done. The New York real estate world is different from the corporate office culture many Americans are used to. It is a very tough business, where you are always looking for a way to make more money, often by sticking it to the other guy. Plus, the usual rules governing how people should behave often don't apply. As a developer, Trump had to negotiate with white collar professionals as well as union bosses, local politicians, and presumably criminal organizations. He had to work with many different types of people and learned the importance of projecting strength. He is far from the only tough-guy New York developer. They're all tough.

Those skills and characteristics are often at odds with how we view our politicians, particularly at the presidential level. We want our world neat and tidy and to reflect the professional world many of us inhabit or aspire to. We want our presidential politicians smooth like John Kennedy and avuncular like Ronald Reagan. Remember how the poor kid Nixon was treated when he was up against the smooth, unflappable, Ivy League Kennedy? He was the ultra-cool Kennedy, while Nixon was the sweaty, striving newcomer.

Trump was more Nixon than Kennedy, and his rival, the smooth Barack Obama, treated him to serving after serving of Ivy League mockery. Obama viewed Trump with utter contempt—with derision and laughter. Even during the 2020 Democratic primary season, billionaire candidate Michael Bloomberg tweeted at Trump, "We know many of the same people in NY. Behind your back they laugh at you and call you a carnival barking clown. They know you inherited a fortune & squandered it with stupid deals and incompetence."

Trump has been the butt of these kinds of insults from his earliest days in Manhattan. There was no hipper publication in those days than *Spy*, a humor magazine run by Graydon Carter, who went on to edit *Vanity Fair*, and his editorial partner, Kurt Andersen. You never met a snottier, more condescending pair. In the pages of *Spy*, they repeatedly referred to Trump as a "short-fingered vulgarian." According to Carter, Trump regularly sends him photos of his fingers with notes like, "See, not so short." Carter says the moniker still gives Trump fits, but like a lot of lefties, he does not understand Trump's humor.

Trump moved to Manhattan to conquer the building trades and get rich. In his twenties, he no longer wanted to be one of the biggest apartment developers in Queens and Brooklyn; he wanted to build landmark buildings in Manhattan. He came with his Queens accent, a chip on his shoulder, a mammoth work ethic, and he always lawyered up. Making it in Manhattan wasn't so easy. He had to wade through a massive and often hostile city bureaucracy, cutthroat competition, and elitist prejudice against a guy from Queens. But despite all the opposition, Trump worked tirelessly to make deals with people who may have hated his guts. He lives for deals and pressed hard to come out of every deal on top. In *The Art of the Deal*, Trump explains that he uses every advantage he can muster. Back then, he was often going up against bigger and richer competitors and, like today, often faced a hostile press and an even more hostile city bureaucracy. We used to celebrate men like that, men who wanted to better themselves and take on the giants. Men like that built America.

Trump made it because he was tough and relentlessly persistent. When he moved to Manhattan, his first apartment was a studio on the East Side with a view of a water tower—hardly the lap of luxury. As soon as he arrived, he promptly called up an establishment called Le Club, a members only restaurant, bar, and nightclub, to request membership. At that time, Le Club boasted a very flashy membership of movie stars, high rollers, and European royalty. They predictably rejected young Trump, who possessed little money and no status. He didn't give up. He became a gadfly to Le Club's management, calling over and over again. They kept rejecting him. He even asked for the membership rolls to "see if there is anyone I know." Finally, Trump lured the head of the club out for drinks at 21 Club, whereupon the head of the club got seriously loaded. (According to Trump, the experience made him realize that his teetotaling would give him an advantage in heavy-drinking New York.) Trump was finally admitted to the club with the proviso that he not hit on any of the young women attached to older men. Trump agreed.

It was at Le Club that Trump met one of his mentors, the legendary attorney Roy Cohn, the *bête noire* of many fevered left-wing nightmares. Cohn famously worked with Senator Joseph McCarthy to go after communists in the U.S. government. Liberals like to forget that Cohn worked closely with Robert Kennedy on the same project. Trump hired Cohn to help him in the government's lawsuit against him for allegedly refusing to rent to blacks in one of his Queens apartment buildings. In what can perfectly sum up Trump's approach to pretty much everything, he told Cohn that he didn't like lawyers because they always want to settle and they never want to fight. Trump always wants to fight and never to give in. He and Cohn sued the government for $100 million. They lost, but the deal they cut—which required Trump to alert the National Urban League of vacancies—was a minor hiccup for Trump.

So much of who Trump is and why some folks don't like him springs from where he came from, how he came up, and how he

succeeded in that kind of business environment. Consider his political incorrectness. He referred to a judge hearing the case against
Trump University as a Mexican. He told a Senate committee that
the owners of an Indian casino "don't look like Indians." He spoke
in a vulgar fashion about women on the *Access Hollywood* tape.
To the Left, these incidents are prima facie evidence that Trump is
a misogynist, a racist, a bigot. People forget that this was how men,
especially men in business, talked as recently as the 1980s. They
also forget that while the educated classes may have changed their
tone, working-class people still speak frankly about topics liberals
have declared off-limits.

William Manchester's seminal memoir of his World War II
service in the South Pacific gives a good portrait of how things were
in the 1980s when it was published. *Goodbye, Darkness* was first
published in 1980, forty years ago, when Trump was making his
rapid ascent through the New York business world and into our
national consciousness. A contemporary reader is shocked at the
stark political incorrectness of those times. *Goodbye, Darkness* was
an undisputed bestseller published by a major publishing house, and
its author was a noted liberal. Still, the book's unabashed use of
"offensive" words and phrases would cancel a career today. For
Manchester, the Japanese are always "Japs" or "Nips." He writes
about a guy looking "like an Arab" and devotes half a page to how
the first man in his unit to die "didn't look Jewish." He does a fair
amount of "slut shaming," calling loose women "whores." He even
refers to Koreans as "termites," a name given them by their Japanese

masters. None of these things would stand today, but they were quite common not so long ago. Back then, casual descriptions like those that Manchester threw around did not indicate some underlying racism. Today, we are oversensitive to these terms. So, when Trump said Indians applying for a casino license "don't look Indian to me," liberals took it as proof that Trump is racist.

The racist label is almost always a cudgel used by the Left against its political enemies on the Right. Sometimes leftists call *each other* racist, sure, like when Elizabeth Warren gleefully called Mike Bloomberg a racist for his successful stop-and-frisk policy. But for the most part, it is an epithet used by the Left against the Right. The Left tends to forget all the statements made by Democrats which would have been labeled racist had they been uttered by Republicans. Joe Biden once referred to Obama as "clean and articulate," and the Left didn't bat an eye. He even said one can't go to a "Dunkin' Donuts or a 7-11 without having a slight Indian accent" before adding, "I am not joking, man." Biden even said black folks "ain't black" if they don't vote for him. Nobody on the Left tried to cancel Joe Biden over those remarks. And when it was reported that Bill Clinton once told Teddy Kennedy that Obama "would be getting us coffee" a few years ago, the media stepped up to defend Clinton.

Trump spent his life on construction sites and has dealt with tough guys all his life (including mobsters). He grew up in a time when there were no "Irish Americans." An Irish guy was simply Irish, or he was a "mick." An Italian guy was not "Italian

American." He was Italian, and often a dago or a wop. We will leave it to the reader to determine if political correctness has been good for our country or not. But it's important to realize that Trump, like millions of Americans, grew up in a politically incorrect world. People traded barbs and epithets without taking things personally, and while the upper crust looked down on it, that still happens today.

■   ■   ■

A lot of Trump's trouble stems from his rivals' willful inability to understand his humor and sarcasm. If you do not get Trump's humor, you don't get Trump. And a lot of the time, Trump opponents deliberately do not "get" his humor in order to attack him.

Trump often makes jokes that poke fun at media narratives. For example, when the mainstream media began to circulate rumors that Russia had hacked the DNC and Clinton campaign, Trump made a harmless joke that would later become the fulcrum for wild conspiracy theories. Bringing attention to Hillary's missing e-mails, thirty thousand of which were curiously deleted after they were requested by a federal subpoena, was a common feature of Trump's campaign rhetoric. Riffing on the Russia stories, Trump told the crowd, "I will tell you this, Russia: if you're listening, I hope you're able to find the thirty thousand emails that are missing. I think you will be rewarded mightily by our press." Trump was *kibitzing*, Yiddish for heckling from the outside.

The media tried to spin the offhand remark into an impeachable offense for over two years. The reaction was instant and long-lasting. One of Hillary's advisers said, "This has to be the first time that a major presidential candidate has actively encouraged a foreign power to conduct espionage against his political opponents." One-time Democratic congressman and former CIA director Leon Panetta said, "I find those kinds of statements to be totally outrageous because you've now got a presidential candidate who is, in fact, asking the Russians to engage in American politics." It was all Kabuki theater depicting Potemkin morals, utterly choreographed and phony. Instead of finding the humor in Trump's comments, the media reverted to despicable pearl clutching.

Dov Fischer, a highly accomplished lawyer and rabbi deeply involved in Jewish and Israeli causes, gave perhaps the best account of Trump's comedic style. According to Fischer, America's Orthodox Jews are the most solid pro-Trump religious or ethnic voting bloc in the country. Fischer, a proud member of the Orthodox Jewish community, claims that support for Trump "runs between 70 percent in radical Los Angeles and 90 percent most everywhere else." He says the support stems "from a deep affinity with his stand on the whole gamut of traditional American cultural and social issues," but that "an underestimated factor is that community's natural acquaintance with Borscht Belt humor." That attunement to Trump's style has given Orthodox Jews an appreciation for Trump's character that few other groups share: "Those who 'get' that humor know precisely how to understand Trump, what to take seriously, what to brush off, and what deeper messages to take away from his speeches and tweets." Fischer explains that Trump can only be understood by realizing that his language, syntax, and pronunciation are pure BQE, straight out of the Brooklyn–Queens Expressway. "Although born to wealth and now even more wealthy," Fischer says, "he also associates with construction workers at his projects, with 'common people,' and naturally talks their talk."

Trump's lexicon and tempo are pure outer borough, a trait he shares with many Orthodox Jews. People were aghast when Trump said that Hillary had gotten "schlongged" by Obama in 2008. In Yiddish, "schlong" means penis, but "schlongged" is neighborhood slang for "stomped." Every real New Yorker knows this. Of course, Hillary did not, but she could hardly be considered a real New Yorker. She carpetbagged to New York in order to get back to Washington, and was in no way a part of the real New York that raised Trump.

Trump rallies attract thousands of fans because they channel that comic energy which Americans love. This is the comedy of old-time comedians like Woody Allen, Mel Brooks, Jackie Mason, and Neil Simon, not the ghostwritten jokes Washington stiffs make. When Trump takes the stage he riffs for an hour or more, and his fans and supporters love it. They howl with laughter and cheer with enthusiasm. But for the elites, who can't admit that Trump knows how to work a crowd, Trump's every word needs to be taken with grave solemnity. Instead of seeing the obvious fun in Trump's remarks, they take him hyper-literally to instill panic. Remember when Trump said, "Maybe I will run for a third term"? To Trump fans, this was hilarious. To the dreary Left it was an attack on the Twenty-Second Amendment and a threat of imminent fascism.

The Left also gets riled up about how he makes fun of his opponents. At this year's CPAC conference, the largest annual gathering of political conservatives, Trump made yuge fun of, well, everyone. He hit one comedic carom shot off of Elizabeth Warren and into Mike Bloomberg. Trump laughed at how Warren went after Bloomberg at Bloomberg's first debate: "He didn't know what hit him. He's going, 'Oh, get me off of this stage.'" And then, to mock Bloomberg's short stature, Trump bent down so you could only see the top of his face over the lectern and in a dying voice said, "Get me off, get me off of this stage." The CPAC crowd went wild. Any Trump crowd would have gone wild. It was hilarious. Broad humor from a president? It's not presidential, the scolds tell us. Trump fans don't care. They love this kind of thing. And Trump knew just what to do. He milked it. He stood there and let them cheer and laugh as he deadpanned them.

Trump's frequent use of over-the-top statements is a good example of his rhetorical style. While these statements may drive liberal fact-checkers crazy, they completely miss the point. Liberal fact-checkers live to correct Trump on even the most minor and irrelevant statements. That attitude fuels claims that Trump has lied some eighteen thousand times since he ran for office. But liberal fact-checkers and the mainstream media hear Trump's claims in a different way than his audience. As a columnist at *The Atlantic* points out, "When [Trump] makes claims…the press takes him literally, but not seriously; his supporters take him seriously but not literally."

While Trump may overstate matters, he does not lie. His audience knows that he's exaggerating and contorting things for dramatic effect. He doesn't mean many of his statements to be taken as fact, as Hillary Clinton did when she said she came under gunfire in Bosnia or Joe Biden did when he said he risked his life to award a soldier a medal in Afghanistan. The proof of this is that while politicians often make false promises, Donald Trump has delivered on the promises he made to the American people.

Trump may make extravagant claims, but he also keeps his promises. For decades presidents have promised to move the U.S. embassy to Jerusalem. None ever did. They probably never even considered it. But while they promised they would move the embassy for decades, only Trump delivered over and against the howls of the rest of the world. Even liberal Jews joined in on the Trump condemnation. Remember when he was called anti-Semitic for saying liberal Jews did not love Israel enough?

In politics, keeping promises is the most reliable and rare mark of a strong character. Politicians say whatever they have to in order to get elected and then proceed to ignore the pledges they made their supporters once they take office. We are told that Trump's character should prevent faithful Christians from supporting him. While he is no paragon of moral virtue, when it comes to politics Trump has delivered on his promises. That is worth more than the fake moral preening for the cameras that obsessed so many of his predecessors.

One noted conservative NeverTrumper actually said that Trump demonstrates bad character by not listening to his advisers. Instead of fulfilling his promises to his supporters, he should genuflect to experts. These commentators think that listening to advisers is a mark of high character. As ridiculous as that may sound, it's one of the central reasons for their personal disdain for Donald Trump. Taking your own counsel over and against that of your advisers, who, as we discussed, are often eggheads with proven track records of screwing the pooch, requires a remarkable amount of courage and fortitude. When Trump trumped the "interagency task force" on Ukraine, the Left and the deep state were outraged. Trump stuck to his guns, because that was the promise he had made to the American people. Was that a sign of poor character?

Some conservative Catholics often repeat these smears against President Trump and his character. In the spring of 2016, Professor Robert George of Princeton and papal historian George Weigel circulated a letter arguing that Trump was manifestly unfit for the presidency because of his supposed lack of character. For the sake of argument, let's agree with their assessment. But should character inform Catholics' deliberations when picking a leader?

Writing in *The Spectator*, Daniel McCarthy argues, "[Y]ou don't select a surgeon based on whether he cheats on his wife; you select him based on whether he's the best person for your specific surgery." McCarthy goes on, "When it comes to a president, the quality that counts is not his goodness as a human being but whether he suits the needs of the country at a given moment."

As Catholics, we make difficult decisions informed by the teachings of our faith. In an increasingly secular world, we cannot expect politicians to share our creed or morals. When we choose leaders, we must think about who can help create a world more friendly to our faith, even if they themselves do not share it.

In 2016, that choice was between a man of obvious personal failings who promised to protect our right to practice our faith and a woman who presented a better public face but was hell-bent on chasing believing Christians from the public square. Voting for third parties or staying home was essentially voting for Hillary Clinton, which, as writer John Zmirak argues, would have been on par with voting for Diocletian over Constantine—that is, voting for persecution over freedom won by a personally sinful man. The choice in the upcoming election will be similarly stark.

You could apply a similar way of thinking to Barack Obama. Obama was considered a model family man and father without a whiff of personal scandal, but he was monstrously evil when it came to public policy. My wife, a lawyer who served on the Clinton impeachment team in the House of Representatives, said of Obama, "He even makes me miss Slick Willie."

When it comes to politics, character means keeping your word. Scores of the Republicans Catholics considered more decent than Trump failed to live up to the promises they made to faithful

Catholics and other Christians. After decades of promises to repeal *Roe v. Wade*, the GOP establishment has barely protested the Left's increasingly radical abortion agenda. Meanwhile, Democrats openly wage war against the tenets of our faith every day. Given the situation, how could a believing Catholic reasonably oppose Trump because of his character?

Lots of Catholics are willing to overlook the key moral teachings of their faith to win the good graces of liberal elites. The *National Catholic Reporter*, in a particularly illustrative example, has published pieces arguing the relative strengths of several Democrat presidential candidates, including Amy Klobuchar, Joe Biden, Pete Buttigieg, Bernie Sanders, and Elizabeth Warren. Each piece quickly and neatly passes over the issue of abortion as if that shouldn't be a deal-breaker for a serious Catholic. But that's not all. None of them mention the assault on the religious freedom of Catholics. Liberals are using all the levers of power to wage war against Catholics and other traditional religious Americans. When it comes to gay marriage, transgenderism, or any other issue where religious doctrine contradicts progressive ideology, the Left feels no compunction impinging on the rights of conscience and religious belief. Astonishingly, one of the writers argues that Pete Buttigieg is the candidate who adheres most closely to the teachings of the Church, despite the much bandied-about facts that Mayor Pete is "married" to another man, says pro-lifers have no home in the Democratic Party, and congratulates children on national television for coming out as homosexual. Even the so-called moderate Joe Biden (who is also a so-called Catholic) often says that transgender rights are the human rights issue of our time. The current party is even crazier than when the McGovern wing took over the Democrats in 1972.

■   ■   ■

Let us close on the question of conversion. Catholics believe in conversion and love conversion stories. One of the most popular programs on EWTN is Marcus Grodi's *The Journey Home*, which is only ever about conversion stories. Has Trump converted? Good question.

At the Family Leadership Summit in Ames, Iowa, Trump famously told the Republican pollster Frank Luntz, "I'm not sure I have ever asked God's forgiveness. I don't bring God into that picture." But then he continued, "I go to Communion and that's asking forgiveness, you know, it's a form of asking forgiveness. When I go to church and when I drink my little wine and have my little cracker, I guess that is a form of forgiveness. I do that as often as I can because I feel cleansed. I say let's go on and let's make it right."

The language of faith is not Donald Trump's native tongue, but it is a tongue he appears to be learning. It's worth noting that Trump didn't claim to be inspired by a great preacher or cherry-picked Bible verses; he is moved by Communion, by the Eucharist (even though Catholics do not believe Protestants actually have the Eucharist). There was something rather Catholic about his statement.

Trump tends to surround himself with Evangelical ministers. It is quite a sight to see him surrounded by them laying hands on him, lifting him up in prayer. Remember when he stopped in at McLean Bible Church to pray for the victims of a recent shooting? Totally unscripted, his hair still matted from golf, the moment seemed completely genuine. While Trump often surrounds himself with Evangelical ministers, he has not built the same public rapport with Catholics. He has not yet appeared at the National Catholic Prayer Breakfast, something George W. Bush did several times (though rumor has it he may yet make an appearance this year), and he has sometimes had a frosty relationship with members of the clergy.

Even so, there is a significant Catholic presence in the White House. During the 2016 campaign, there were so many practicing Catholics on the team that staffer Katy Talento, later to oversee healthcare issues on the Domestic Policy Council, organized a daily rosary. The Trump administration is manned by many a devout Catholic. Former acting chief of staff Mick Mulvaney was a practicing Catholic, as was Andrew Bremberg, who headed the Domestic Policy Council and is now U.S. ambassador to the United Nations in Geneva. White House Counsel Pat Cipollone, a daily communicant, was the former top legal counsel to the Knights of Columbus. One of the president's top speechwriters, Brittany

Baldwin, is a Numerary (celibate) member of Opus Dei. Without a doubt, she was the one who wrote his magnificent speech for the March for Life. To this day, an Opus Dei priest from the nearby Catholic Information Center presides over Masses in the Indian Treaty Room that boast a healthy attendance.

And there is abundant evidence that Trump himself has come a long way on his faith journey. On Ash Wednesday, President Trump released a statement unlike any other in recent memory. In the statement, Trump talked briefly about Ash Wednesday and what it means, that it is a time for fasting, praying, and engaging in acts of charity. And then he said this: "This powerful and sacred tradition reminds us of our shared mortality, Christ's saving love, *and the need to repent and accept the gospel fully*" (emphasis added). When I read the statement, that last part shocked me. In this secular age, in which some would say the unofficial state religion is closer to paganism than Christianity, such blatant evangelization is remarkable. When did George W. Bush, George H. W. Bush, Ronald Reagan, Richard Nixon, Bill Clinton, Barack Obama, or even Jimmy Carter ever make an official pronouncement as audacious as this? They all boasted their Christian bona fides, but they never defended the faith as strongly as this.

Christians often compare Trump to a range of figures from sacred history. Some compare Trump to Constantine, while others compare him to the Old Testament David. One writer compared him to Samson, God's appointed judge over Israel, who was given to lying, deception, and disobedience. Samson dallied with prostitutes and was a womanizer. Needless to say, he was not exactly a role model approved by Israel's mothers and fathers. And even though Samson was chosen by God, he tended to violate the promises he made to God.

Against the will of both God and his parents, Samson chose the wrong woman, who proceeded to sell him as a slave to his enemies. In captivity, Samson was treated like an entertaining clown. His captors strung him between two temple pillars, mocked him, and ridiculed his lack of strength, which his wife Delilah had taken away from him. But in a flash his strength returned, and he pulled down the temple on his enemies, killing more of them that day than he had ever killed before.

The story of Samson teaches that God has a plan, and that sometimes he chooses someone we consider to be the wrong vessel. It is not for us to judge the actors God has chosen, and sometimes they might surprise us.

Trump's critics find such comparisons delusional and sometimes offensive. And while some may go too far in drawing parallels between Trump and biblical heroes, the general point still stands: God often works through men and women who are not exemplars of piety. As Catholics, we don't need to believe that Trump was divinely appointed in order to see him fulfilling the divine mission. According to Church teaching, not even the pope is appointed by God. (God inspires those who chose the pope, but they are free to reject His inspiration.) Still, the comparison points to the fact that we do not know the full story and will not know until the Final Judgment, when all things are revealed.

CHAPTER TWO

Trump and Abortion

There are lots of reasons for Catholics to embrace Trump the man, but none of those reasons would mean a lick if the Trump administration hadn't advanced the most pro-Catholic agenda in recent memory. Trump has stuck to his guns on policy, delivering his promise to faithful Christians. As the Trump campaign likes to say, "Promises Made, Promises Kept."

It is likely that no policy issue matters more to devout Catholics than ending abortion. For years, we've fought the secular powers waging war on the unborn, who are without a proper champion in Washington. At first, Trump looked shaky on life issues, leading several Catholic academics and activists to issue an appeal to their fellow Catholics to reject Trump. As we've already mentioned, dozens of notable Catholic academics and intellectuals drafted and signed letters opposing Trump. In their missive, Professor Robert

George of Princeton and papal biographer George Weigel took issue with Trump's character, which they called "manifestly unfit" for our nation's highest office. Besides their attack on his character generally, the letter warned that "there is nothing in his campaign or his previous record that gives us grounds for confidence that he genuinely shares our commitment to the right to life."

Lots of pro-life Americans shared similar concerns. Before the 2016 Iowa caucuses, ten high-profile pro-life women issued an open letter telling Iowa voters that Trump could not be trusted. Pro-lifers, they counselled, should vote for anyone else but him. Pro-life activists warned that the evangelical leaders who had already endorsed Trump—a growing list that already included Jerry Falwell Jr. and former vice presidential candidate Sarah Palin—were playing with fire. One of the letter's signatories, Marjorie Dannenfelser, president of the Susan B. Anthony List, expressed surprise that faith leaders would endorse Trump without assurances that he was genuinely pro-life.

At that time, it was not unreasonable to wonder whether Trump would advance a pro-life agenda. Though he had paid lip service to the pro-life cause, Trump had given some suggestion that he didn't view it as a particularly high-priority policy item. He was on record saying that his sister, a New Jersey federal judge who had struck down a partial-birth abortion ban, would make a good Supreme Court justice. He had even said that he would consider pro-abortion Massachusetts senator Scott Brown for vice president.

So, skepticism was understandable. After all, pro-lifers had been fooled before. It was forty-three years into the abortion regime, and *Roe v. Wade* stood firm. Victory seemed still far from our grasp, and here some were considering a man with no pro-life record over candidates who were true-blue pro-lifers, including Senator Ted Cruz and former senator Rick Santorum.

Wringing empty promises from politicians' mouths sometimes seemed like the pro-life cause's only accomplishment. Since *Roe*, anyone running for president as a Republican, indeed almost anyone running for office as a Republican, has had to say he is pro-life. But most of the time, those words never travelled from the campaign trail to elected office. Ronald Reagan told us he was pro-life and then went on to nominate Sandra Day O'Connor, a vociferous defender of abortion. George H. W. Bush said he was pro-life and then nominated David Souter, another reliable vote for the abortion regime. George W. Bush did better, but even his nomination record is less than sterling. While he nominated Samuel Alito, for whom we have great hopes, to our nation's highest court, he also nominated John Roberts, who has caused conservatives grave concern. And that's just his confirmed nominees. Despite being a born-again Christian, W. tried to nominate the sketchy Harriet Miers before he was stopped by pro-lifers.

Republican presidents couldn't even get their nominations right, over which they have tremendous control. How could they promise to do anything to defund Planned Parenthood, which still receives billions in federal funding to this day? In fact, most GOP candidates have been supporters of the abortion giant. And these were presidents who boasted long track records of supporting our cause. Trump, meanwhile, had no pro-life credibility to stand on. In fact, he had advocated for abortion in the past.

In 1999, when Trump ran for the Reform Party presidential nomination, he voiced the typical lefty Catholic "personally-opposed-but" view to NBC's Tim Russert. "I hate the concept of abortion. I hate it," Trump told Russert. "I hate everything it stands for. I cringe whenever I hear people debating the subject. But I still believe in choice. I am strongly for choice and yet I hate the concept of abortion." Trump chalked up his pro-choice views to living in New York for his whole life, making sure to note that New York is different than Iowa.

Twelve years later, Trump considered running for the GOP nomination. If he was to have a shot at coming out of primary season alive, he knew his view had to change. Trump claimed his view had changed "years ago." He told the 2011 Conservative Political Action Conference that he was "pro-life." He said the same to Laura Ingraham on Fox News. And in an interview with David Brody on the Christian Broadcasting Network, Trump recounted the story of his change in perspective. "A friend of mine's wife was pregnant," Trump began, "and he didn't really want the baby.... He ends up having the baby and the baby is the apple of his eye. It's the greatest thing that's ever happened to him. And you know here's a baby that wasn't going to be let into life. And I heard this, and some other stories, and I am pro-life." In the next election cycle, that story would become a constant in the Trump repertoire. In classic Trump fashion, the child turned into a "superstar," while Trump was now "very, very proud to say that I am pro-life."

Personal experience can transform people's moral opinions, but there was still reason to remain skeptical about Trump. Some pro-lifers thought he was a wolf in sheep's clothing, "just another phony pro-lifer trying to become president on the GOP line."

Despite nearly half a decade recounting his change of heart, Trump faced mounting evidence that his story was just that—a story. When a 2013 interview with satellite radio provocateur Howard Stern was revealed, Trump's critics came out of the woodwork in full force. Stern had pushed hard, asking Trump, "Are you really anti-abortion? You're not. I know you're not. There's no way."

"I mean, I feel certain ways about things, and is it a priority for me?" Trump responded. "Because my priority has always been China and jobs. Somebody asks me, and I say pro-life," Trump said. "But it's never been an issue that really has been discussed with me in great detail."

But as soon as Stern began to do exactly that, Trump's pro-life views disappeared.

"Do you really believe government should be regulating what a woman's personal decision is?" Stern asked.

"Of course not," Trump replied.

It's always good to take Howard Stern interviews with a grain of salt, but it's clear that when these tapings took place, Trump's views were still in a tangle. Back then, his pro-life professions weren't backed by any real conviction. Never mind the language of faith; even pro-life words are far from his native tongue.

During the 2016 campaign, Trump went on to make much stronger pro-life statements. At the third presidential debate he told Chris Wallace that late-term abortion should be illegal. In the CNN-Telemundo debate, he said he would defund Planned Parenthood. He said that abortion should be illegal except in cases of rape, incest, or to save the life of the mother.

But Trump still made missteps, and lefty Catholics waited for his slipups with bated breath. They would chuckle about how conservative Evangelicals and Catholics were being duped by the Orange Man. Shortly after his announcement in June, he told former Democrat staffer Jake Tapper that he was "pro-choice." Catching himself, he said, "I'm pro-life. I'm sorry."

His inexperience in discussing abortion was on full display when he told Chris Matthews that women who have abortions should be punished. Abortionists have fever dreams of pro-lifers putting women in jail for murder and threatening women who have natural miscarriages with hard time. Before the segment even ran, the Trump campaign corrected the record, writing that if abortion were made illegal, "the doctor or any other person performing this illegal act upon a woman would be held legally responsible, not the woman." Trump had found a movement pro-lifer who knew the intricacies of the issue, and he let him speak.

But then a few days later, he veered in the opposite direction. He told CBS News that the abortion laws were set. "At this moment, the laws are set. And I think we have to leave it that way." Statements like that are the equivalent of Supreme Court nominees declaring that they consider *Roe v. Wade* "settled law." In response, the Susan B. Anthony List said Trump had "disqualified himself as the GOP nominee." (It's worth noting that Susan B. Anthony president Marjorie Dannenfelser had signed a letter along with other pro-life women condemning his candidacy.)

The Trump campaign corrected him almost immediately, using some communications gymnastics to bring Trump back in line. They said the law will stay the way it is until he becomes president. Once in office, Trump "will change the law through his judicial appointments and allow the states to protect the unborn. There is nothing new or different here."

All these zigs and zags happened over the course of three days in March and April 2016. The *Washington Post* described it as "5 different positions on abortion in 3 days." No wonder some Catholics viewed Trump with skepticism.

Trump's heavy abortion baggage and his scattershot comments not only demonstrated a lack of knowledge on the life issue, they also made him look like a hustler. Leftist Catholics ridiculed gullible pro-lifers for believing another lying Republican once more.

But in a stroke of genius, Trump called on the help of faithful Catholic Leonard Leo of the Federalist Society to right the ship. In the months leading up to the election, Trump and the Federalist Society teamed up to publish a list of judges from which he pledged to choose his Supreme Court nominees. As we all know, fixing the judiciary is the key to overturning *Roe v. Wade* and outlawing abortion. Some didn't trust Trump's word, but the pledge assuaged the concerns of many Catholics. And we were right to believe him.

But even if we didn't trust Trump, where else would we have gone? The November election approached, and pro-lifers had nowhere else to go. It was Trump or bust. Pro-lifers certainly could not vote for Hillary, for whom abortion is practically a religious sacrament. Bill's abortion mantra was "safe, legal, and rare," but Hillary and her bloodthirsty supporters wanted limitless, government-funded abortion on demand. Plus, the late, great Antonin Scalia's Supreme Court seat was up for grabs, and the next president was certain to pick a number of Supreme Court justices. We had to throw in our lot with the one who seemed the most likely to do the right thing.

My view at the time was two-fold.

First, I did not believe he cared two bits about the abortion issue on either side. It was not anything he had ever cared about, either in favor of abortion or against. I suspect he was nominally pro-choice, if he ever thought about it. But he was not doctrinaire.

But, second, and this was key, he also did not care about the approval of the *New York Times*, *Washington Post*, or the cocktail circuit in Washington, D.C. Consider that a marginal talking-point pro-lifer in the Oval Office could very well bend to establishment approval every time, if he cared about that sort of thing. At the time, Trump might have been a mere talking-point pro-lifer, but he also did not care what the elites thought of him. He thought he was better than them anyway. Therefore, my view was that he would end up doing what movement pro-lifers wanted. He would, as they say, dance with those "who brung him." This view has been borne out in what eventually happened in his first term. In short, he has been the most pro-life president in history.

Start with personnel. There is an old saying in Washington that "personnel is policy." By appointing a veritable all-star team of pro-life personnel, Donald Trump has done the most for the pro-life cause. Unfortunately, most pro-lifers remain unaware of these accomplishments since they often amount to "inside baseball." And while I can't say that I know the full extent of the pro-lifers scattered through the federal bureaucracy, I know that there are many political appointees advancing the pro-life cause every day.

It would harm the cause if I revealed all that I know on this score. Make no mistake, the other side knows who the pro-lifers are in the administration. But they do not know all the details of what senior officials have in the works. I'll divulge those details to the extent that I can.

Let's start with the White House.

Andrew Bremberg, the head of the president's Domestic Policy Council, is a movement pro-lifer. Bremberg is a graduate of Ave Maria University and the Catholic University of America School of Law. When he headed the Domestic Policy Council, he played a large part in scuttling the first effort by leftist bureaucrats to put abortion in a Security Council resolution. If it had been adopted, the motion would have placed a right to abortion in the very heart of international law. In later congressional testimony, Bremberg admitted he had a hand in stopping the Security Council resolution, proudly bearing witness to his pro-life views.

"Abortion is not the answer to any moral question," Bremberg told the Senate Committee on Foreign Relations. "I believe life begins at conception and ends at natural death."

To my knowledge, no nominee for federal office has ever given such a stark answer to a question about the right to life. Most nominees, even those who say they are pro-life, dissemble, saying, "Well, I have strong personal views, but I will follow the direction of the president and carry out his policies." Instead of standing for their beliefs, they give an oily and cowardly response to their inquisitors. Bremberg, to the contrary, flies his flag high. So, flustered by his blunt and unexpected answer, rabid pro-abortion senator Jeanne Shaheen said he was stonewalling. When I heard that, I laughed out loud. Shaheen had never heard such a straightforward and honest answer, and she didn't know what to do about it.

Bremberg's director of health policy was Katy Talento, who had previously worked as a Senate staffer for one of the most pro-life senators in history, the late Dr. Tom Coburn of Oklahoma. An expert on insect-borne diseases in Africa, she also happens to be a movement pro-lifer. Prior to coming to the White House, she had published articles condemning contraception. Imagine the bravery required to touch the third rail of public policy! She came under severe attack when she was appointed to the White House. While in that key White House spot, Talento spent long nights working on multilateral negotiations around the world and played a central role in nixing the abortion code words "reproductive health" from international agreements, among many other things.

Let's be clear: the term "reproductive health" was invented by the Left as code for abortion. It has appeared in hundreds of UN documents and has become part of the pro-abortion argument in the law of the world. But, thanks to pro-life people in the White House, the United States Agency for International Development (USAID), the Department of Health and Human Services (HHS), and the State Department, this president has become the first one to fight it tooth and nail. George Bush, for instance, did not even contemplate fighting against it.

A lot of Trump's high-profile staffers are Catholics dedicated to the pro-life movement. Plus, scores of pro-life Catholics and Evangelicals can be counted among the hundreds working in the White House and the nearby Eisenhower Executive Office Building.

Communications specialist Kellyanne Conway, also a Catholic, played a central role in advancing the pro-life cause at the White House. Conway was deeply involved in the movement for years. She had even been a regular presenter at a secret quarterly meeting of pro-life leaders in Washington, D.C. Even Steve Bannon, whom elsewhere I have called a "non-practicing orthodox Catholic," was in the White House. Though never of the movement, he was nonetheless a true-blue pro-lifer. There have even been pro-life Catholics in senior roles at the National Security Council who have intervened in a pro-life way at G-7 negotiations.

Go through the other branches of the executive branch and you'll find many more. Eric Hargan is a faithful pro-life Catholic who is deputy director, the number two person, at the Department of Health and Human Services. Roger Severino runs the civil rights office at HHS and has played a role in religious freedom and conscience protection. Severino has hired an all-star pro-life team for his staff, including Valerie Huber, formerly a campaigner for abstinence education; Shannon Royce, formerly of the Family Research Council; and Arina Grossu, also from the Family Research Council. David Christianson, who ran government relations for the Family Research Council, works in HHS government affairs. Matthew Bowman, who came from Alliance Defending Freedom, is deputy general counsel at HHS. March Bell, a longtime government official and supporter of the pro-life and pro-family movements, was Severino's chief of staff. Longtime pro-life and pro-family activist Charmaine Yoest was there for a time. The list goes on, but it's worth noting that so many pro-lifers are in senior positions at the Department of Health and Human Services, an agency that has been dedicated to advancing the abortionist agenda in Democrat administrations. Flipping the script and using the tools available to HHS to defend life will have repercussions for decades.

But even with a cadre of faithful Christian pro-lifers as large, dedicated, and talented as that assembled by the Trump administration, lasting change is difficult to accomplish. Political appointees are up against a stone wall of permanent staff who stand on the other side of the issue. While it's certainly possible to advance the cause of life and family at government agencies such as HHS, the opposition is immense and well entrenched. Even government bureaus largely unknown to the public are firmly dedicated to the liberal social project. USAID, the government's overseas development office, is the chief font of all sorts of culture war nastiness in foreign countries. USAID ships hundreds of millions of dollars to foreign countries to implement UN-style "family planning." As if that weren't enough, USAID imposes a hard-left sexual ethos on aid recipients, promoting sexual orientation, gender identity, and transsexualism propaganda around the world.

I mention this example because USAID is not an organization the average American citizen knows about, let alone associates with the Left's culture war. When Democrats are in power, the full force of government is at work advancing leftist abortion policies and gender politics. When Republicans are in office, there are a few brave souls there who do their very best to stem the tide. I will not report on all of them because many of them work under the radar, but there are those in top jobs who are sympathetic to the cause of life and family. They are surrounded and can only advance the cause at the margins. But they do.

Bethany Kozma is one administration official who deserves comment. Kozma is a young mother and Evangelical who is among the bravest people you will ever meet. She has served as a senior official at USAID throughout the Trump administration, but it wasn't easy for her to keep her job after the Left tried to tar and feather her. Several years ago, Kozma made a two-minute speech at the Fairfax County (Virginia) School Board opposing the then-new transgender policy that was implemented against massive opposition from parents. She also published a column at The Daily Signal on the same topic. For these quite mild interventions, the Left came for Kozma's scalp, calling her a "violent anti-trans extremist." Nonetheless, as senior adviser on women's issues at USAID, she has played a key and highly effective role in UN negotiations on life issues. In recent days, Kozma has been promoted to deputy chief of staff at USAID, where she will be working closely with William Steiger, another pro-lifer with years of experience on these issues.

While the Left failed to take down Kozma, they have gotten scalps at the State Department. Mari Stull, an experienced trade expert, was named to a senior role in the Bureau of International Organization Affairs; she resigned within months after she came under extreme pressure from the deep state for her strong pro-life actions. Stull was instrumental in ensuring that State Department negotiators held the Trump line against "reproductive health" in UN negotiations. Her boss, Ambassador Kevin Moley, who headed the bureau, was chased out for the same reason.

Pro-life sentiment goes all the way to top at the State Department. Secretary of State Mike Pompeo has been a reliable pro-lifer throughout his career, dating back to his years in the U.S. House of Representatives. Sources tell me that his two chief advisers, men he has known since his days at the U.S. Military Academy, are also true-blue social conservatives. Even Pompeo's top aide on Iran, Brian Hook, is a faithful Catholic and thoroughly pro-life. Hook, too, has come under extreme pressure from the social liberal deep state but, so far, has not succumbed as Stull and Moley have.

Remember, personnel is policy. While Trump has appointed top people in key posts from the ranks of the pro-life movement, many of whom are either Catholic or Evangelical and deeply sympathetic to the cause, what have they accomplished? Let's start with foreign policy.

Previous presidents who claimed the pro-life mantle often suffered from a lack of imagination. They seemed reluctant to do anything pro-life or anything that would upset the pro-choice establishment. Upon taking office, Republican presidents were content to do two things. First, they would defund the UN Population Fund, the UN agency that is complicit in establishing the Chinese one-child policy. Second, they would reestablish the so-called Mexico City policy, a Reagan-era policy that bans certain American money from supporting organizations overseas that perform or promote abortion. I say "certain American money" because the Mexico City policy stopped money from flowing from the relatively small "family planning" budget only. American dollars still flowed to these groups, but from other, larger parts of the federal budget.

These moves were often enough to satisfy the major pro-life groups. Talk pro-life, promise good justices (but never any who pledge to overturn *Roe*), defund UNFPA, reinstate the Mexico City policy: if a GOP president did these things, he would get rubber-stamped by the major pro-life advocacy groups. Would he move against Planned Parenthood? Not a chance. Would he aggressively fight a global right to abortion? Maybe on the margins, but he was more likely to take George W. Bush's course of action and sacrifice all that to his other foreign policy initiatives.

Like his predecessors, Trump defunded UNFPA and reinstated the Mexico City policy. He did so on his first day in office, but that was just the beginning of his pro-life actions, not the end.

Although the Mexico City policy traditionally affected only the part of the federal budget that funded "family planning," Trump expanded the ban to include the much larger health budget in foreign operations. He increased the ban from roughly $600 million to nearly $9 billion. Two years later, in March 2019, Secretary of State Pompeo announced that the government would also block what he called "backdoor funding schemes and end-runs" around the ban. Overseas groups would no longer be allowed to pass money through to subcontractors who supported or performed abortions. On that same day, Pompeo announced the revocation of funding to the Human Rights Court of the Organization of American States because personnel from the court had been caught lobbying for legal abortion in South America.

Trump is even taking on the United Nations, which actively supports abortion overseas, by threatening to defund the most controversial parts of the UN apparatus. The decades-long fight to prevent the UN from establishing a global right to abortion has been one of the pro-life movement's greatest battles. Abortion advocates at the UN know they cannot explicitly impose abortion on the world, so they work to establish what is called a "customary right" to abortion. A customary right is established when all countries agree to change their behavior without signing a document. By abstaining from paper documents, member states don't have to ratify treaties that might spark outrage at home.

For years, the Left has tried to turn the repeated, vocal agreement by UN member states into something akin to a treaty obligation. To do so, they've invented "customary rights," hoping to give greater authority to the repeated references to "reproductive health" in UN documents. This is a key argument of the abortion Left and must be fought vigorously if we are to prevent UN bureaucrats from establishing a global right to abortion. Starting twenty-five years ago, "reproductive health" has been included in nearly everything the United Nations does. If you read UN documents, you'll find the term in almost every proposal, from those dealing with housing and children to women and the environment.

The move to include abortionist language in every nook and cranny of UN policy has gone on for decades. The Clinton and Obama administrations joined the European Union and other member states in pushing hard for "reproductive health" in UN documents. George W. Bush was lukewarm at best in fighting use of the term. Instead of fighting "reproductive health," the Bush administration fought against "reproductive health care *services*," arguing that "services" alluded to abortion. But even a casual follower knows that "reproductive health" always includes abortion, regardless of whether or not "services" follows in the text. Fighting for minutiae doesn't absolve the Bush administration's catastrophic decision to allow a commitment to "reproductive health" to enter into the first and only hard-law treaty, the Convention on the Rights of Persons with Disabilities, in December 2006.

The great sea change at the UN has been the Trump administration's refusing to go along with the "reproductive health" consensus. He has opposed reproductive health not only at the UN but also at the G7 and other international fora. United States diplomats have been ordered to strike the term out of any agreements with foreign nations. Should they fail, they are to replace it with something acceptable, such as "maternal health," or if they are unable to do that, they have to add a provision explicitly excluding abortion from "reproductive health." By making "reproductive health" controversial again, Trump and his team have successfully stemmed the tide of those calling for a global right to abortion.

Fighting UN resolutions may seem small, but the UN offers vast sums of money to countries around the world. Lots of that money comes from American taxpayers, meaning that if the United Nations starts supporting organizations promoting "reproductive health," American citizens are ultimately on the hook. Taking the fight to the United Nations is another attack on the liberal abortionist agenda and makes it more difficult for the war on the unborn to spread abroad.

There are certainly more funding holes to plug, but the Trump administration has demonstrated an unprecedented commitment to ending U.S. taxpayer–funded abortion abroad. Pro-lifers who work on foreign policy are hopeful more cuts will come, despite the fact that Trump has already accomplished much more than any previous president on this score. He seems dedicated to the cause and to continuing to go beyond the bare minimum required to win over the pro-life vote.

As we have discussed at length, not caring what the elite think is one of Donald Trump's great strengths. The global pushback on expanding the Mexico City policy and fighting "reproductive health" has been immense, incurring blowback from political leaders and the international press alike. The elites considered abortion promotion settled policy, decided in the backrooms of the UN where hardly any American pays attention. Ignoring the pro-abortion policies of international institutions would have been easy. But instead of taking the easy route Trump has worked to do the right thing, and there is more to come.

■   ■   ■

Over the past decade, pro-lifers in the States have passed more pro-life laws than at any other time in our history. They have focused most on ensuring the safety of patients: requiring abortionists to have privileges at the local hospital, requiring abortion clinics to meet the same physical plant standards as other surgery centers, and requiring parental notification and waiting periods. The result of many of these laws has been the shuttering of abortion clinics. Some states have only a single abortion clinic.

As important as these advances have been and as angry as they have made the abortion Left, there is still *Roe v. Wade* that ensures abortion on demand in all fifty states, which means this is ultimately a matter for the courts. And hope remains very high since Trump has been able to appoint dozens of judges to the lower courts. By the end of 2019, he had appointed 133 district court judges out of a total of 677 and 50 appeals court judges out of a total of 179. This on top of two new Supreme Court judges. By the end of the second term, Trump's true legacy might be a complete overhaul of the federal judiciary.

Consider what he has done in one nutty circuit court, the Ninth Circuit based in San Francisco, a longtime bastion of left-wing craziness and the most overturned circuit court in the country. Trump is on track to appoint fully half of the sitting judges there. He has done this largely by ignoring the wishes of California Senate Democrats, who have traditionally had a kind of veto power over picks to the Ninth.

As always, the proof of the pudding is in the tasting. Conservatives have appointed judges that seemed solid but who perhaps lied during the process or otherwise became disappointments. One of the differences with Trump is that judges must be able to prove with a past record that they are conservative-minded.

One of the disappointments right out of the box was when the Supreme Court, including Gorsuch and Kavanaugh, voted with the lower courts in denying the right of states to ban Medicaid abortion payments to the poor. We shall see if they have the stuff to actually overturn *Roe*. We certainly hope so.

There are a number of cases working their way through the lower court and bearing down on the Supreme Court, including fetal heartbeat bills that ban abortion after a heartbeat is detected. There are numerous state bans on abortion after the twentieth week of pregnancy. Early in 2020, the Trump administration asked the Supreme Court to uphold a Louisiana law requiring abortionists to have admitting privileges at the local hospital. Practically any one of these could be the vehicle to overturn the abortion regime at the federal level.

What we know for certain is that the *New York Times* was dead wrong in January 1973 when it announced that the *Roe* and *Doe* decisions had "settled" the abortion question. Here we are decades later, and there is nothing as unsettled in our law and policy as federal abortion law.

■   ■   ■

Planned Parenthood is the largest and richest abortion provider in the United States. Every year, Planned Parenthood commits more than 300,000 abortions—and that number continues to grow even though abortion is in decline nationwide. That means Planned Parenthood is getting a greater market share in a declining market, and the United States government is helping them do it.

According to a Live Action analysis of Planned Parenthood annual reports, in the year 2000 Planned Parenthood performed 197,070 of the 1.3 million abortions in the United States, putting their market share at 15 percent. That same year, they received $202 million in government funding. By 2018, Planned Parenthood had performed 345,672 abortions of less than 862,320 in the country, giving the organization a whopping 40 percent market share. And Planned Parenthood brought in $616 million from state and federal government sources.

Candidate Trump was all over the map with regard to Planned Parenthood. He praised them. He condemned their abortion business but seemed to fall for the canard that their abortion business is only 3 percent of their total services. He said he wanted to defund Planned Parenthood, but only their abortion business. But Trump did become the first GOP standard-bearer to announce he would defund Planned Parenthood. Pause over that. No previous GOP candidate ever promised to defund Planned Parenthood.

The Trump administration has taken several positive actions to fight Planned Parenthood's abortion-on-demand business model. The Justice Department announced an investigation into Planned Parenthood's baby-parts business, in which the organization was charged with selling aborted baby organs to medical and scientific researchers in seeming violation of federal law. But there was other good pro-life news out of the Department of Health and Human Services. In June 2019, the department announced the cancellation of a massive contract for taxpayer-funded experimentation with body parts from aborted babies. The cancelled contract was with the University of California, San Francisco. Susan B. Anthony List president Marjorie Dannenfelser, whose group had been campaigning against the funding, said, "This is a major pro-life victory and we thank President Trump for taking decisive action. It is outrageous and disgusting that we have been complicit, through taxpayer dollars, in the experimentation using baby body parts."

Given Congress's militant opposition to defunding Planned Parenthood, the Trump administration has been forced to fight the abortion lobby dollar by dollar with regulatory changes. In January 2018, the Trump administration reversed an Obama rule that prevented states from blocking local Planned Parenthood branches from receiving federal Medicaid dollars, the largest single source of government funding flowing to Planned Parenthood. The rule change was hotly contested in the federal courts as activist groups lined up to sue the federal government on account of the change. But instead of cowering from the mob of activists, the Trump administration held firm, defending their power to change the rule. Ultimately, thanks to the administration's stalwart legal defense of the change, the courts sided with the states that want to defund.

In February 2019, the Department of Health and Human Services announced the Protect Life Rule to direct so-called Title X family planning money away from the abortion industry. Planned Parenthood refused to comply with the new rule that would have prevented it from referring for abortion. As a result, it lost $60 million, the first time Planned Parenthood lost federal funds. Though the total sum amounts to a drop in the bucket for the corrupt organization, a win is still a win and shows President Trump's commitment to stemming the abortion tide.

Though pro-lifers have been disappointed with the amount of money Planned Parenthood continues to receive from state and federal sources, no previous president has ever taken aim at Planned Parenthood, and certainly not with the intensity of the Trump administration. George H. W. Bush's father, U.S. senator Prescott Bush, was so supportive of Planned Parenthood that he was nicknamed "Rubbers." His son George H. W. and grandson George W. were no less supportive of the abortion giant in their actions, though they may have made rhetorical appeals to the pro-life movement.

But as every pro-lifer knows, the state is only part of the problem. Public opinion and rabid liberal interest groups are just as powerful a force in propelling the abortion regime forward. Planned Parenthood receives millions of dollars in private donations and benefits from news coverage that borders on advertisement. In that context, President Trump's greatest accomplishment has been making Planned Parenthood controversial again. And this is reflected in a changing attitude toward what has traditionally been a sacrosanct group.

Public perception is changing on Planned Parenthood. Thanks to this administration's actions, people are starting to realize that the propaganda surrounding the organization is just a cover for its murderous operations. That change is affecting Planned Parenthood's ability to conduct its bloody business. In its latest annual report, Planned Parenthood was forced to admit that it lost a whopping 400,000 donors in the 2018–2019 fiscal year.

So, when a Catholic asks if Trump shares the Church's view on abortion, we believers are entitled to ask whether that matters. At this point it is almost irrelevant whether Trump holds the Catholic view on abortion. In fact, we know he does not. In his mind, the government should allow exceptions for rape, incest, and the life of the mother. But Trump's actions are more relevant than his beliefs, and while this chapter is hardly exhaustive of the work he and his personnel have undertaken, the groundswell of pro-life initiatives in all the federal departments is reason enough to give President Trump our full support.

To sum up, pro-life Catholics should rally around President Trump for two reasons. First, he has put movement pro-lifers in key roles. Those pro-lifers have dug into the nitty-gritty of the regulatory apparatus that makes abortion possible. Second, Trump is not afraid of elite opinion. Throughout the pro-life movement's history, we have been hamstrung by politicians who solicit our support just to cave to their liberal masters at the mainstream cultural institutions. President Trump has proven impervious to that group's pressure, which means he has the courage to put bold proposals forward. In a word, Trump is the most pro-life president we have ever had.

CHAPTER THREE

Trump and Religious Freedom

There are two large areas of religious freedom we should be concerned about: the disaster happening overseas and the chipping away that occurs here in the United States. President Trump and his team are engaging both.

The Catholic Left has a tendency to mock Christian conservatives for their concern about domestic religious freedom precisely because it does not rise to the level of what happens in, say, Nigeria, where murderous Islamists target whole villages of Christians, torturing and killing them. And this is certainly true, but the fact that we are not being murdered for our faith does not lessen the serious attack we are undergoing from our own government and from the Left.

At home, religious freedom used to be a unanimous bipartisan project. You may not know that, and it is certainly hard to imagine at this divisive remove. Consider this: the Religious Freedom

Restoration Act was introduced in the House of Representatives in March 1993 by leftist Democrat Chuck Schumer of New York and in the Senate by Ted Kennedy of Massachusetts. It passed unanimously in the House and very nearly unanimously in the Senate, and it was signed into law by President Bill Clinton. That is how noncontroversial the issue was only a few decades ago.

And then came the rise of the homosexual movement and the claim that religious freedom was a mask for religious bigotry. Things changed practically overnight. I have spoken to congressional staffers who were in the room when the religious freedom coalition of Democrats and Republicans broke down and disappeared. And that is where we are now. To gays and their supporters, religious freedom is now bigotry that they must eradicate.

Every religious American knows that under the leadership of Barack Obama the federal government became decidedly hostile to the practice of Christian faith. When President Trump was elected to our nation's highest office, he was charged with the task of recovering the America that promoted religious faith rather than silenced it. Christians in America faced an unprecedented situation in our history. The homosexual advance leading up to and following the imposition of gay marriage on the country by *Obergefell* meant that the government was willing to interfere in our private faith lives to an unprecedented degree. Instead of defending our rights, the United States government sought to drive us from the public and even the private square.

The gay agenda has been based on deception from the get-go. For years, gay activists insisted that same-sex marriage would not have a negative effect on religious believers. They pledged it would not extend beyond the nuptials between two men or two women. This, of course, was utterly false. They knew it then, and the rest of America has subsequently learned it.

The debate over homosexuality and anti-discrimination law began in Massachusetts in 1989, when a bill passed prohibiting discrimination based on sexual orientation in public and private employment, union practices, housing, and public accommodation. The new law raised questions of spousal benefits and parental rights, specifically foster care and adoption by homosexual couples. While same-sex marriage was not even suggested in the law, discerning observers knew it was the first battle in what would prove a long campaign to fundamentally change American society.

At the time, Catholics heard what would soon become a familiar refrain. We were assured that changes in access to public services would have no impact upon Catholic institutions. When religious folk raised justifiable concerns, gay activists and liberal tastemakers responded with biting mockery. Many went as far as to suggest that our concerns were borne out of our own insecurity with our own heterosexuality. They tried to shame us into submission, and in Massachusetts, it worked.

When that law passed, the liberal activists were predictably emboldened. Unsurprisingly, they chose to fight similar legal battles advancing the gay agenda in the same state. In 2004, same-sex marriage was imposed on the state of Massachusetts by the state high court. Massachusetts became only the fourth jurisdiction in the world to countenance same-sex marriage. Homosexual activists again insisted this would have no impact on Catholic institutions.

It only took two years for the state to break its promise to Catholics. In 2006, Catholic Charities was informed that it now had to place adoptive children with homosexual couples. Faced with the possibility of endless discrimination lawsuits, the organization had to choose whether it would stay in the adoption apostolate and violate its sacred mission or close its doors. The Boston Archdiocese chose the latter, and later that year the Archdioceses of San Francisco and Washington, D.C., followed suit. Illinois Catholic Charities also closed its adoption doors. Bishop Thomas Paprocki of Springfield said, "In the name of tolerance, we are not being tolerated."

Bishop Paprocki clued into the new stakes in the culture war. With gay marriage, the Left started to ruthlessly enforce its new moral vision on the rest of the country. Even though there were many other adoption avenues for same-sex couples, the leftist bullyboys needed to make an example of traditional organizations that dared to dissent from their vision. Using the Trojan horse of tolerance, the Left smuggled their new absolutist morality into our legal system. At the time, it was all rather new. But today, with gay marriage legal nationwide, Americans are now familiar with the dreary parade of small businesses being hounded with endless lawsuits by gay activists insistent that there be no dissent from their sexual orthodoxy. The best known is the Masterpiece Cakeshop dispute featuring a brave man named Jack Phillips.

In the summer of 2012, two men entered Jack Phillips's cake shop and asked him to create a unique wedding cake for their same-sex wedding. Phillips, who specializes in custom cakes, told them that his faith prevented him from contributing to their "marriage" celebration with a cake designed specifically for their wedding, but that they were free to buy any premade cake in the store. The men stormed out with vulgar words and gestures. Within an hour of the incident, Phillips was harassed with threatening phone calls, protesters, and news crews. He didn't know it then, but his cake shop had just become the center of the national debate on the limits of religious freedom in the face of the sexual revolutionaries.

Phillips was brought before the Colorado Civil Rights Commission, where he faced a $500 fine and a year in prison for refusing to celebrate a same-sex wedding with his professional artistic expertise. Without any evidence whatsoever, the commission determined that Phillips's objection was less about religious freedom than his hostility toward homosexuals. According to the commission, Phillips used religious freedom to hide his nasty prejudice, despite the fact that Phillips had been nothing but courteous to the men.

Diann Rice of the commission was quoted as saying, "Freedom of religion has been used to justify all kinds of discrimination throughout history, whether it be slavery, whether it be the Holocaust, whether it be—I mean, we—we can list hundreds of situations where freedom of religion has been used to justify discrimination. And to me it is one of the most despicable pieces of rhetoric that people can use to—to use their religion to hurt others."

Rice's view is shared by many on the Left, many of whom would have stood for religious freedom before the rise of the LGBT movement. Martin Castro, Obama's pick to chair the U.S. Commission on Civil Rights, once said religious freedom is often used as a code word for discrimination, intolerance, racism, sexism, homophobia, Islamophobia, and "Christian supremacy."

Phillips was ordered to retrain his staff to ensure compliance and to file quarterly reports with the government detailing his efforts to comply with the order. The decision against Phillips was upheld by the Colorado Court of Appeals, and the Colorado Supreme Court refused to hear further appeal. Phillips and his lawyers took his appeal to the U.S. Supreme Court, where he won, but the ruling was unsatisfactory. Rather than explicitly saying that a Christian business owner may not be forced to participate in a morally objectionable transaction, the Court said the commission's decision was based on religious animus, as shown by the comment of Diann Rice. Phillips was deemed innocent, but no precedent was set, exposing Phillips to the threat of future lawsuits.

And that's exactly what happened. Just a few days after the Supreme Court decision, the sexual revolutionaries targeted Phillips and his bakeshop again. A "transsexual" tried to get him to bake a cake celebrating his sexual "transition." This clear harassment has led to further legal proceedings and litigation. Jack Phillips seems to have spent more time in the courtroom than in his beloved cake shop. In our crazy time, he really is a Christian martyr bearing witness to the faith.

Jack Phillips was not the first case of the government's using the force of law to enforce its sexual ideology, and he certainly will not be the last. Christians face something of a new state religion, one that is hostile to Christianity. The new religion seeks out heretics and uses the new black-robed priesthood, judges, to punish them. Its adherents will not rest until they root out people who believe in the moral teachings of their faith. They'll try to humiliate anyone who crosses them, whether it's an organization as large as the Catholic Church or as small as Masterpiece Cakeshop.

The gay rights campaign was just the latest in a string of attacks Democrats launched against Christians. Under President Obama, government officials targeted Catholic employers with lawsuits for violating contraceptive mandates. Much like Jack Phillips has begrudgingly become the poster child for resisting the advance of the gay agenda, the Little Sisters of the Poor now represent the fight against tyrannical contraceptive policies.

For those who don't know the story, the Little Sisters of the Poor is a Catholic congregation that cares for the indigent elderly in their dying days. After the passage of Obamacare, the organization objected to the new requirement to provide contraceptives and abortifacients in their healthcare plans. When the rule initially came out, the Obama administration denied the Little Sisters a religious exemption even though Obama had allowed exemptions for thousands of secular employers. The government claimed that the Little Sisters of the Poor didn't qualify because their apostolate ministers to those outside the Catholic faith. By that standard, religious organizations that do any evangelizing or outreach to nonbelievers don't deserve religious protection, even when caring for others of different faiths is a core tenet of religious belief. As Cardinal William Keeler of Baltimore once said, "We do not teach the inner-city kids of Baltimore because they are Catholic, we do it because we are Catholic." Yet, according to President Trump's predecessor, caring for the poor elderly who might be Jewish, or Protestant, or atheist is not Catholic at all. As a result, the Obama administration threatened the Little Sisters with crippling fines if they did not comply with the new regulations.

In this context, one in which Democrats weaponized the levers of power at their disposal against dissenters from their disordered sexual morals, the first political priority for Christians was to stop the bleeding. Four more years of any Democrat in our nation's highest office would result in a significant advance of the Left's moral crusade. The domestic persecution of religious believers has happened almost exclusively at the hands of Democrats. Though some Republicans may privately applaud the suppression of Christian views, they would likely never use state power to root out Christianity. The Left certainly will, as the Obama administration demonstrably proved.

While any Republican is almost certainly preferable to a Democrat in this regard, President Trump has taken extraordinary measures to protect and advance the cause of religious liberty. Where the Obama administration used the administrative state to sue churches unwilling to comply with his moral vision, President Trump has directed his subordinates to advance the cause of religious liberty. On May 4, 2017, Trump issued the executive order "Promoting Free Speech and Religious Liberty." This early executive order would set the tone for Trump's time in office. As the president himself said, under his watch, "The federal government will never ever penalize any person for their protected religious beliefs."

Since then, religious liberty initiatives have come in droves. Five months after President Trump issued his executive order, the Department of Justice followed suit with a new report that promised to review new regulations for compliance with the Religious Freedom Restoration Act. Federal agencies had long ignored the religious liberty statutes that are on the books, confident that their liberal friends in the federal government would never hold them accountable for violating the First Amendment rights of American citizens. Thanks to President Trump's directive, the Department of Justice will ensure that will not happen again.

Early in 2018, the Trump administration announced the formation of the "Conscience and Religious Freedom Division," an enforcement office in the Department of Health and Human Services. The purpose was to meet the growing threat to the religious freedom of healthcare workers who are being forced to participate in abortions. Even medical students were being pressured to learn how to perform abortions. The threat against conscience rights became even more acute with the rise of the transgender movement. Is an ob-gyn required to treat a "transgender woman," i.e., a man in a dress who may have been surgically altered to at least somewhat resemble a woman? What's more, would a doctor be forced to assist a man who wants to resemble a woman by cutting off his genitals or prescribing puberty blockers or cross-sex hormones?

As one could expect from any Democrat executive, the Obama administration became very aggressive in cutting back conscience protection. Within months of taking office, Obama moved to overturn a Bush administration policy that allowed healthcare workers to decline to participate in any medical service that violated their beliefs.

Christian conservative Roger Severino, who runs the Office for Civil Rights of Health and Human Services, said, "[W]ith the launch of this division, you do not need to shed your religious identity; you do not need to shed your moral conviction to be part of the public square."

In January 2020, Trump announced administration-wide protections of religious believers. Chief among the protections was the overturning of an Obama order requiring faith-based social service groups—healthcare entities, child welfare agencies, and educational nonprofits—to disclose their faith mission to clients. Obama also required these groups to refer clients to other secular groups. These secular groups, meanwhile, were not required to announce their secularity or to refer to faith-based groups. See how unfair that is?

Obama and his team intended to use this as a scarlet A around the neck of do-gooder Christian groups and set them apart. Christians in Obama's America had to play by different rules. President Trump changed that.

Further Trump changes included beefing up protections for students who want to pray in school. The Trump administration is reminding all schools that students and teachers have a constitutionally protected right to pray in school and to have access to school facilities just like secular groups. In the Oval Office when Trump announced these changes, a Catholic student stood next to him who said a teacher had forced him to wipe away ashes from his forehead on Ash Wednesday. A Christian girl was present who said her school in Texas had told her she had to pray in private.

These assaults on religious belief and practice will return in a future Democratic administration. While Barack Obama was a watershed moment in the culture war, future Democrat administrations will certainly make him look like a moderate on social issues. The 2020 Democratic primary proved that the party is all in on the culture war. Today, the abortion industry and the LGBT movement are the two most powerful constituencies in the Democratic Party. They contribute hundreds of millions of dollars to the Democratic Party and will expect further assistance in stamping out Christian resistance.

President Trump can't protect Christians forever. Opponents of religious freedom are rich and powerful, and they have the sympathetic ear of all the power centers in our society.

Government, business, and the academy are all working to advance the Left's social mission. This administration has done its best to give us the tools we need to practice our faith without harassment. We need four more years to ensure that the gains we've made last a little bit longer.

If you think that the Left is going to relent in their moral crusade, you're simply mistaken. While we fight over gay marriage and abortion, the Left has already moved on to a new, more dangerous culture war battle. Now, they want to redefine gender.

Transgenderism is the developing battle conservatives will have to win in order to protect the religious beliefs of millions of Americans. The gender debate has startling consequences for men and women. It attempts to define the primary facts of human life out of existence. It will take a Herculean effort on behalf of the Justice Department and strong-willed and strong-stomached prosecutors and judges to resist the tide of gender insanity. Any Catholic who cares about doctors, nurses, children, and a proper understanding of human sexuality must look with gratitude to the Trump administration for not caving in to this new ideology.

■   ■   ■

Religious freedom is not only under attack domestically. There are savage attacks on religion and religious believers around the world, and Donald Trump is far and away a champion on this issue internationally.

In January 2020, four students were abducted from a seminary in Nigeria. At this point in the Middle Belt region of Nigeria, a war against Christians had been raging. Thousands had been killed, with thousands more being burned out of their homes at the hands of Muslim Fulani herdsmen. In the northeast of Nigeria, Boko Haram and the Islamic State of West Africa had been terrorizing Christian villages.

Aid to the Church in Need believes upwards of 327 million Christians are persecuted around the world. That is roughly the population size of the United States. The group Open Doors USA told the website Crux that 245 million "experience heavy persecution in the top 50 countries where it is most dangerous to be a Christian."

Dede Laugesen, executive director of Save the Persecuted Christians, told Crux, "[T]error groups promoting sharia supremacy are growing, and increasingly coordinating activities across northern Africa and the Sahel," which is a belt stretching all the way from the Atlantic Ocean to the Red Sea just below the Sahara Desert. She cites bloody persecution of Christians in Nigeria, Niger, Chad, Cameroon, Burkina Faso, and Mali, mostly at the hands of Islamic radicals. She cites Islamic advances in Somalia, Uganda, Mozambique, and the Democratic Republic of the Congo.

Without a doubt, recognition of this problem was also once a bipartisan issue. The International Religious Freedom Act of 1998 may have been initiated by Republicans, but it was supported by Democrats and signed into law by Bill Clinton. The law created an ambassador at large on the issue and an office in the State

Department that would issue an annual report on religious persecution. And this report named names.

The annual report would cite the countries of "particular concern," and then the State Department would attempt to work out an agreement with the targeted country. Early on, Vietnam was designated a "Country of Particular Concern." The United States negotiated a binding agreement whereby Vietnam would no longer enforce "forced renunciation of faith," would release all known religious prisoners, and would allow hundreds of churches to reopen.

Unfortunately, a hiccup occurred during the Obama administration. The LGBTs quite literally imposed themselves into the Office of International Religious Freedom in the State Department. What do LGBT issues have to do with religious freedom abroad? Good question. When some of the employees of the office complained, they were removed. One of them is Emilie Kao, who now works on these issues at the Heritage Foundation.

President Trump has reinstated the original purpose of promoting religious liberty abroad. Religious liberty is no longer subordinated to the interests of the gay lobby; it's now an explicit priority of American policy. Under previous administrations, the ambassador for religious freedom reported to mid-level management at the State Department. Under Trump, the ambassador reports directly to the secretary of state. This markedly elevates the issue in the eyes of the State Department and of countries around the world.

Trump made a spectacular appointment when he named former Kansas senator and governor Sam Brownback to the post. A Catholic convert, Brownback has been known his whole career as a vocal and enthusiastic supporter of social conservative issues. Though an elected official, Brownback has practically been a movement social conservative. He packed his Senate staff with hard-core pro-life and pro-family advocates.

To make their commitment to religious liberty loud and clear, the Trump administration hosted two high-profile summits on the topic. In the summers of 2018 and 2019, the State Department convened upwards of one hundred governmental ministers from countries dedicated to the religious freedom article of the UN Charter. Hundreds of civil society groups participated in what were the first such meetings in U.S. history.

On the opening day in 2018, Vice President Pence said, "The list of religious freedom violators is long; their crimes and oppressions span the width of our world. Here in our own hemisphere, in Nicaragua, the government of Daniel Ortega is virtually waging war on the Catholic Church. For months, Nicaragua's bishops have sought to broker a national dialogue following pro-democracy protests that swept through the country earlier this year. But government-backed mobs armed with machetes, and even heavy weapons, have attacked parishes and church properties, and bishops and priests have been physically assaulted by the police."

He cited China: "Farther from home, but close to our hearts, religious persecution is growing in both scope and scale in the world's most populous country, the People's Republic of China. The State Department's annual International Religious Freedom report has labeled China as a religious freedom violator every year since 1999. Together with other religious minorities, Buddhists, Muslims, and Christians are often under attack."

Pence warned that Jews in France and Germany are now routinely told not to wear the Kippah, also known as the yarmulke, because it makes them easy targets. In 2012, four children were murdered outside their Jewish school in Toulouse. In 2016, terrorists assaulted a Parisian kosher supermarket.

Pence toured the world with horror stories of religious persecution. He announced a program called the Genocide Recovery and Persecution Response Program that would "closely partner with local faith and community leaders to rapidly deliver aid to persecuted communities, beginning with Iraq."

The Left was particularly incensed when pro-life and pro-family law professor Mary Ann Glendon of Harvard was appointed to head the State Department's Commission on Unalienable Rights in the fall of 2019. Though the office of the secretary of state insisted the commission would not be about abortion and gay marriage, the only un-unalienable rights discussed at the international level are the "human rights" to abortion, sexual orientation, and gender identity. Conversely, the Commission on Unalienable Rights is trying to clarify the true meaning of human rights while removing the ridiculous rights introduced into international charters by the sexual Left.

It is abundantly clear that religious freedom and freedom of conscience are in surer hands today under the Trump administration than under the previous administration. It's also clear that a vote for Joe Biden is a vote to return to promoting the Left's sexual politics abroad under threat of military force. Any Democratic administration would continue the persecution of Christians around the world for taking their beliefs on human sexuality into the public square. In order to make the world safe for homosexuality, they would eradicate Christianity as we know it.

If President Trump does not win his re-election bid, the Left will accelerate its attacks on Christians at home and abroad. That is not a matter of speculation: they have promised to do so themselves under the guise of fighting "discrimination." There is a war on religious believers, and its fighters include powerful players in the federal government. This is what we face if Trump is not reelected.

With Trump in office, we can expect continued protection from the federal government. While that may be worth a great deal, it's not particular to this administration. Any Republican would make sure the administrative state doesn't go after Christians. Donald Trump in particular, however, has worked to ensure that the religious liberty protection he provides believers will continue after he leaves office. With another four years of the Trump administration, Christians will see the gains President Trump has won us enshrined in law.

CHAPTER FOUR

Trump and Judges

I once sat with Justice Antonin Scalia at a prayer breakfast at a Times Square hotel—not the rough, dirty, old Times Square, which the jokester Scalia said he preferred to the new Disney-fied Times Square we see today. As we sat together having breakfast waiting for him to talk to the crowd of six hundred or so, a woman approached and verbally petitioned him on *Roe v. Wade*. When she left, Scalia said that in a better world, no one would know who he is.

What Scalia meant is that the Supreme Court ought not to be at the center of our political lives as it has become in recent decades. It would be a mistake to think that *Roe v. Wade* alone elevated the role of the Court. Certainly, things have intensified since January 1973, but the Court had become a combatant in the culture wars a few decades prior to that when it removed prayer from schools. Then it struck down state regulations on contraception, which paved the way for the Pill and the whole sexual revolution that followed behind.

Still, it was the abortion case that made the justices household names and their nominations and Senate confirmations so central to our political lives. *Roe v. Wade* put the increasing relevance of the court into hyperdrive. Since the 1973 ruling, pro-life Catholics have had high hopes that the decision would be overturned either by the Supreme Court or through a constitutional amendment, neither of which has materialized. But, since then, Republican candidates and Republican presidents have promised "strict constructionists" or "originalists," who naturally would vote to overturn the nebulously decided *Roe v. Wade* that was found nowhere in the Constitution but only in the fevered mind of Justice William Brennan and another four of our black-robed masters.

Because we have been fooled so many times by these promises, similar promises from Donald Trump were met with a great deal of skepticism, particularly since he said his federal judge sister would make a good Supreme Court justice even though she has voted to uphold partial-birth abortion. And everyone knew Trump's evolution on abortion was of recent vintage and not entirely believable.

The courts are important, and Catholics have been burned before. The unexpected death of Justice Antonin Scalia on February 13, 2016, well and truly roiled the political waters. The earthquake that was Scalia's death caused a tsunami on all sides of the political spectrum. Every conservative pro-lifer knew where he was when

Scalia's death came through the newswire. We froze. Obama was president, and we had lost one of the most influential conservative justices in our history. He could have been replaced by a rabidly pro-choice abortionist.

As is well-known, Senator Mitch McConnell rebuffed Obama's nominee Merrick Garland, refusing to give him consideration and therefore kicking the decision to the next president, who could have been any one of a number of Democrats and Republicans running.

Some experts thought Scalia's death could well scuttle Trump's run because he could not be trusted on judges. His opponents kept hammering him on the comments he made about his liberal sister. But at an Iowa GOP debate, Trump shocked everyone by naming potential nominees, something previous candidates had been loath to do. They'd mention the usual strict constructionist blather and might praise Scalia, as George W. Bush had done, but they never named names. Always unconventional, without an establishment set of consultants telling him what to do, Trump named names. The two he named—William Pryor and Diane Sykes—warmed the cockles of conservative hearts.

That went so well that Trump decided to put together an actual list from which he promised to pick the next nominee. According to Mollie Hemingway and Carrie Severino in their masterful retelling of the Kavanaugh battles, *Justice on Trial*, "To get on the list, a judge (1) had to adhere to an originalist and textualist judicial philosophy, (2) had to have a clear record of following that judicial philosophy, and (3) had to have demonstrated the courage of his convictions—criteria that reflected a determination to avoid the failures of previous Republican presidents."

Working with congressional supporters and Leonard Leo of the Federalist Society, along with input from the Heritage Foundation, on May 18 Trump produced a list of eleven names, a veritable wrecking crew of excellent picks, though neither Neil Gorsuch nor Brett Kavanaugh were on the initial list. Trump referred to the list as "potential" nominees, implying he might pick a name not on the list. This set off alarm bells. Here was the GOP Supreme Court hustle once again. In September, he put out a longer list and promised it was the list he *would* choose from. Again, this had never been tried by any previous presidential candidate.

Replacing Scalia with a liberal would have been a disaster. When Senate Majority Leader Mitch McConnell stalled Obama's pick, the Democrats were spitting mad. Some of his colleagues might have gotten wobbly, but McConnell held firm and made this pick an important part of the presidential campaign. And it was this issue of the federal judiciary that helped get Trump elected. Within a few days of his inauguration, President Trump nominated Neil Gorsuch.

Many naysayers contend that any GOP president would have picked from the same list that Trump used. They contend Trump himself did not create the list, the Federalist Society did. All this may be true, but here's the thing: Trump's opponents argued that Trump would appoint liberal justices. Even after he produced the list, they said Trump was lying. Hardly anything he said was believed in certain quarters, especially when it came to abortion. But he did the right thing. He did the pro-life thing. And there is an increasing chance that sensible pro-life restrictions can be upheld and that *Roe v. Wade* can be overturned at some future date. None of this would have happened if any Democrat, and especially Hillary Clinton, had been elected. And by the way, no president actually produces the list of potential nominees. They all have advisers, often the wrong ones. Trump listened to the right ones.

A year later, in the summer of 2018, a second earthquake hit Washington, D.C., when Justice Anthony Kennedy announced his retirement. Kennedy was the result of perhaps the worst political development in the latter days of the twentieth century. The Democrats' butchering of Judge Robert Bork led to an aborted appointment of a judge named Douglas Ginsburg, who had to withdraw when it was revealed he had smoked pot with his law students. Next up was Anthony Kennedy. As always, proponents assured us he would be a reliable pro-life vote. His wife worked in a crisis pregnancy center, after all. Nothing could have been further from the truth. Kennedy became a reliable abortion vote, going so far as writing what has come to be known as the "sweet mystery of life" passage in the *Planned Parenthood v. Casey* decision that upheld and even more firmly entrenched the abortion regime in American jurisprudence. Kennedy was an utter disaster for social issues, including not just abortion but man–woman marriage.

Since Kennedy was a reliable abortion supporter, replacing him with a pro-lifer would potentially swing the Court firmly into the pro-life camp. Justices Samuel Alito, Clarence Thomas, John Roberts, Neil Gorsuch, and Brett Kavanaugh potentially supported overturning *Roe*, while Elena Kagan, Sonia Sotomayor, Stephen Breyer, Anthony Kennedy, and Ruth Bader Ginsburg were all in favor of abortion rights. Losing Kennedy could move the court from 4–5 against life to 5–4 in favor of life.

It is now well-known that President Trump nominated Catholic Brett Kavanaugh to replace Kennedy. Over spurious charges of sexual assault as a teen, the nomination turned into a surreal nightmare for Kavanaugh and the nation. What strikes many of us is how firmly Trump stood by his nominee. Trump is a fighter, and he unleashed Kavanaugh, who went on to make one of the most impassioned political speeches we have ever heard in a confirmation hearing. We wondered if someone like Jeb Bush would have been quite so strong in his defense of Kavanaugh, or if he would have caved and quietly suggested to Kavanaugh that he step aside. Trump never even considered it.

Some have argued persuasively that *Roe* won't be overturned until the Supreme Court becomes 6–3 or even 7–2. On this most controversial issue, justices would feel more comfort in a crowd, albeit a small one, than being the fifth vote to overturn *Roe*. Pro-lifers are within a whisker of that sixth vote. Every day we hear about the cancer struggles of eighty-seven-year-old abortion radical Ruth Bader Ginsburg, who seems to be hanging on simply to prevent Trump from getting another appointment to the high court.

Waiting in the wings is Judge Amy Coney Barrett, also a Catholic, a circuit court judge, and a professor at Notre Dame University School of Law. Quite famously, during a hearing for Barrett's current judgeship, Democratic senator Dianne Feinstein of California said, "The dogma lives loudly within you." Catholics loved it. Experts argue it will take a woman to replace Ginsburg. But you can be sure, even a woman will come under prolonged vicious attack from the pro-abortion Left, for whom abortion is practically a sacrament in their new church. We can expect the Left to go after Barrett in ways we cannot even now imagine.

■   ■   ■

Donald Trump's successes do not just come at the Supreme Court. When Donald Trump was elected to America's highest office, he had the opportunity to reform the entire federal judiciary by appointing conservative judges. While this may seem easy enough, the issue is decidedly more complex. Though paying much lip service to originalist jurisprudence and organizations like the Federalist Society, Republicans have a mixed record when it comes to picking the right judges for the federal court. Their failures make Donald Trump's accomplishments especially notable.

In this day of divided government where one party may control the White House and another one or both houses of Congress, it is very nearly impossible for the president to put any kind of semi-permanent stamp on public policy. Sure, President Obama managed to do that with his Affordable Care Act, but that was dishonestly rammed through the U.S. Senate, where his party held a sixty-vote supermajority. For the most part, presidents rely on new rules and regulations promulgated in executive branch agencies and executive orders to advance their policy priorities. President Obama went as far as to brag about his "phone" and his "pen," asserting that he did not need Congress to turn the country to the left. True enough. But those who live by the phone and pen almost certainly die that way.

Executive action can easily be undone when an administration has the will to change policy. We already mentioned Trump's decision to overturn the the Mexico City policy in his first days in office, but there are dozens of other examples. Obama signed the United States on to the Paris Climate Accord without congressional consent, so Trump had no problem pulling the United States out almost immediately upon being elected. Obama unilaterally joined a multilateral deal with Iran and never asked Congress. As he was warned at the time by Senator Tom Cotton, this, too, was undone with the flick of a pen by President Trump.

President Trump has also had to rely on executive action to achieve his goals. Just as we saw with Obama, those policies can be overturned on day one of an incoming administration. Perhaps the only enduring way for presidents to put their stamp on public policy is through the Court and its lifetime appointments. The picking of federal judges and justices to the Supreme Court is thus of paramount importance. At their best, judges, with life tenure, can police the bounds of what kind of executive action is authorized by Congress. At their worst, judges, who never face the voters, can drive policy themselves beyond what is authorized by the law and Constitution.

The conservative view of the courts is mostly defensive: We need judges who will not legislate from the bench to advance progressive policy items. We also need enough room to maneuver the administrative state when we do hold power. Practically any legislative or executive advance by a conservative Congress or administration is immediately challenged in the courts, and often in courts the Left already knows will be sympathetic. Different federal courts have different ideological makeups, and interest groups tend to sue the federal government in courts they assume are most friendly to their cause. In a practice known as forum shopping, plaintiffs find the right venue that will provide the right judge to hear the case. This is why so many suits against Trump seem to originate in Honolulu, or San Francisco, or Seattle, or even Eugene, Oregon. Of course, conservatives often do the same thing: states like Texas would file their cases in Wichita Falls to halt Obama-era policies.

Those courts have significant power to determine the administration's actions. Left-wing judges now engage in the ahistorical practice of issuing national injunctions, preventing the government from executing policy it's resolved to enact without giving a ruling. That's how a single judge in Hawaii, for instance, can halt an administration against not just the plaintiff in Hawaii but anyone anywhere in the United States or even abroad. Because the action has been halted, the injunction bars the Department of Justice from defending it in other courts.

The courts are therefore crucially important for issuing new rules and regulations, the main way a president can defend his policy agenda. But they're also important for the culture war, as activist judges use the courts to strike down conservative laws.

For several decades, Republicans have lost just about every culture war battle through the courts. There's some cause for that. While Democratic presidents appointed wildly ideological judges, Republicans held the ingrained belief that they could not insist on so-called "litmus tests." Long-standing practice is to refuse to ask where a candidate stands on the right or wrong reasoning of *Roe v. Wade*, or even the morality of *Roe*'s result. Conservative candidates for the high court insist that they cannot comment on cases that may come before them—not to the Senate or the president. In the past, this was probably because establishment Republicans simply didn't want overtly "anti-abortion" nominees hung around their necks.

The Democrats are not so hampered. They insist—even loudly—that their candidates pledge fealty to a "woman's right to choose" as well as a host of other political issues. Democrats choose candidates who are proud defenders of the abortion regime. While recent Democrat Supreme Court picks such as Ruth Bader Ginsburg and Elena Kagan refused to tell the Senate what they thought about *Roe*, they were nominated after decades of political work (at the ACLU for Justice Ginsburg and the Clinton and Obama White

Houses for Justice Kagan) making it abundantly clear what they thought. And recent Democratic candidates like Hillary Clinton and other leading Democrats all insist they will impose an overt litmus test.

The conservative approach to the judiciary is fundamentally different. Judges, as Chief Justice Marshall said centuries ago, exist to say what the law is. This means that they are *not* super-legislators enacting their policy preferences; they are applying the law and Constitution as written. Typically, the terms used for this are "textualism" with regard to statutes and "originalism" with regard to the Constitution. Again, in stark contrast to the liberal goal of reaching judicial results apart from the legislative process, textualism and originalism are based on the principles of democracy and limited government. Textualism means that when elected representatives pass a law, that law means the words on the page at the time of the law's enactment. If you want them to mean something different, elect new legislators and pass a new law. It's the same with originalism: if you want a constitutional right, it had better be in the text of the Constitution as originally understood by the framers. If it isn't, you need to amend the Constitution.

Conservative thinking on this has developed over the years. For many decades, Republicans wanted "judicial restraint" as opposed to "judicial activism." The idea was that "restrained" judges would not see themselves as senators in robes, but would defer to the elected branches. Republican presidents, therefore, should find "modest" judges and not "activists."

This approach provided mixed success, at best. Indeed, politically left-wing Catholics have made great hay over the fact that it was Republican-appointed justices who both wrote the *Roe v. Wade* decision imposing abortion on demand and also upheld it twenty years later. The liberal Catholic canard is that the GOP does not really care about abortion, except insofar the issue is never resolved so that the rubes will continue voting for the ersatz pro-life party. Their Supreme Court picks prove it.

While the Republican Party certainly has its fair share of failures, claiming that Republicans are insincerely pro-life goes too far. Republicans failed in their nominations to the judicial bench because they didn't properly diagnose the problem with judicial liberalism. While conservatives thought the problem was the activism and thus positioned themselves against reading policy positions into the law, the real problem was the Left's lawlessness.

I have no doubts that Justices Sandra Day O'Connor, Anthony Kennedy, and even David Souter were sincerely opposed to "judicial activism" when nominated for the Supreme Court. Indeed, that misguided sense of "restraint" caused them not to upset the *Roe v. Wade* applecart. The distinction between "restrained" and "active" misunderstands the role judges play in our legal system. It's to be correct in applying the law. The change from disposition (restraint/activism) to methodology (textualism/originalism) reflects an understanding among Republicans that their judicial picks need to do more than not legislate from the bench.

Conservative legal philosophy adapted to these challenges. Organizations such as the Federalist Society came to realize that "stealth candidates," or nominees without a record of conservative jurisprudence, were dangerous. They would often use the right "dispositional" language when under consideration for appointment and then rule in favor of the most egregious decisions with their liberal colleagues once named to the position they sought.

This lesson—no more stealth candidates—has been taken to heart by the Trump administration. Former associate White House counsel Robert Luther has written about judicial interviews under Trump. He says they are "modeled after the Justice Scalia law clerk interview, although the Scalia law clerk alums in my former office have said that our interviews are even more intense." He explains, "In prior Administrations, judicial candidates were often interviewed by phone, by one Associate Counsel in a fifteen minute pro-forma interview, or not at all. In this Administration, the hundreds of judicial candidates that we have considered were personally interviewed at the White House by White House Counsel's Office and Department of Justice Office of Legal Policy staff." It is a process that could be described as "No More Souters."

While selecting good judges is hard, getting them confirmed is even harder. This is a lesson learned painfully during the Bork hearings. Ronald Reagan picked the right guy when he nominated Judge Robert Bork, who was one of the most powerful intellects in American legal circles at the time. Based on qualifications alone, he should have been a shoo-in for the Supreme Court. But by that time, *Roe v. Wade* had changed everything in judicial politics. In the old days, justices were confirmed with large majorities. And before that, justices did not even have hearings in the Senate. Now they do have hearings, and those hearings better resemble a professional wrestling match than the sober actions of the world's greatest deliberative body.

The circus of judicial nominations all started with Bork. Here was a man who was a top judge on the second-most influential court in the country. He was a Yale professor, a former solicitor general, and a partner at the famed Kirkland & Ellis firm. He personally revolutionized how judges look at statutes, the Constitution, and even antitrust. Yet Senator Ted Kennedy insisted the dark night of fascism would descend if Bork were confirmed to the Court. Kennedy implied that women would be forced into back-alley abortions and Jim Crow laws would magically be revived. Republicans were simply unprepared for this kind of slander. Just months before, Justice Scalia, certainly as conservative as Bork, had puffed on his pipe during his hearings before the Senate confirmed him 98–0. What happened? The fight against Bork was coordinated by the Left, and liberal activist groups took to the airwaves and to the streets to gin up opposition to Judge Bork. It was a well-orchestrated hit job designed to protect abortion on demand. In the end Bork was defeated, and his consolation prize was having his name become a verb for vicious leftist attacks before the Senate. He had been "borked."

Conservatives learned the lesson, coming to terms with the new tactics the Left would use to defend its judicial hegemony. When the Left went after Clarence Thomas with spurious charges of sexual harassment made by a former colleague, the charges were rebuked. The move was straight out of the Bork playbook. The same interest groups and senators tried to make as much of a public spectacle as possible in the hopes that the Republicans would back down. As a result, Clarence Thomas is a Supreme Court justice, and Joe Biden—who ran the shameful Thomas hearings—has failed in all of his previous presidential campaigns.

Unfortunately, the attacks aren't limited to Supreme Court nominees. The Left knows full well that lower-court judges can be just as effective at undermining its social engineering, and a federal bench full of conservatives means an excellent "farm team" for the Supreme Court. Better to stop them from becoming judges at all than wait to have to fight them at the Supreme Court level.

In recent years, we've seen ample evidence of the campaign against Republican nominees to the lower courts. Take the case of Amy Coney Barrett. A well-respected tenured professor at Notre Dame Law School, Barrett had clerked for Justice Scalia and was appointed by Chief Justice Roberts to serve on the Appellate Rules Committee. A devoted mother of seven who seemed to "have it all," she was an obvious pick to serve on the U.S. Court of Appeals for the Seventh Circuit in Indiana. But you could see the Democrats react in real time: Mother of seven? At Notre Dame? She must be one of *those* Catholics. At her hearing before the judiciary, Professor

Barrett came under vicious attack by the Democrats, and the line of attack was a clear violation of the constitutional protection against religious tests for higher office. Senator Dianne Feinstein said Barrett's Catholic faith was a "concern" and then uttered the now-famous phrase, "The dogma lives loudly within you." This became a rallying cry for faithful Catholics across the country. Illinois Democrat Richard Durbin asked if she considered herself an "orthodox Catholic" and whether she liked Pope Francis. Outside groups, à la the Judge Bork and Clarence Thomas hearings, circulated rumors to the *New York Times* that she belonged to a dangerous religious cult. But Republicans stood firm, and Barrett was confirmed. She is now a hero of the grass roots and a front-runner for any future Supreme Court openings.

Catholics aren't the only ones who get slammed. In August 2019, another Trump circuit nominee, Steven Menashi, was attacked by leftist commentator Rachel Maddow for being an alleged racist because he had supposedly written a law review article calling for "ethno-nationalism." It was explosive. But was it true? Menashi, a law professor and former law clerk to Supreme Court justice Samuel Alito, was writing in an Ivy League law journal about the right of Israel to guarantee citizenship to Jews. It turns out that Menashi's family is of Babylonian Jewish origin and was driven from Iraq by a murderous pogrom called the "Farhud," so he takes the existence of Israel as a safe haven for the Jewish people rather seriously. Despite liberal efforts, he's now Judge Menashi.

In September 2019, Sarah Pitlyk was nominated for a federal district court in Missouri by President Trump. A former law clerk to Brett Kavanaugh, Pitlyk, a Yale Law School grad and public-interest litigator, was attacked for her advocacy of pro-life views. Pro-abortion Democrat Richard Blumenthal of Connecticut told her, "You've been more than just an advocate for the anti-choice agenda. You filed a brief arguing that life begins at conception. You've defended Iowa's abortion ban. You worked to defund Planned Parenthood." She pointed out an inconsistency in the Democrat position, saying, "I stand in a long line of other people who have sat at this table who have had history in advocacy, or in an issue-related advocacy, or in politics and who have become very distinguished jurists." This was likely a specific reference to the sainted Justice Ruth Bader Ginsburg, who made her career at the ACLU's Women's Rights Project prior to becoming a judge. Pitlyk was also confirmed by the Senate.

Perhaps the most remarkable fact about these controversial nominees is not that they were selected, but that President Trump stood by them when they were smeared. Trump critics like to say that any old Republican president would have picked Neil Gorsuch and Brett Kavanaugh for the Supreme Court. You name a Republican president, and he'll listen to the Federalist Society and the Heritage Foundation when it comes to judges. Perhaps. Any Republican president would surely hear out judicial conservatives when picking a justice, but they also would have listened to the bevy of advisers and courtiers they'd have accumulated in years—or decades—of government service. Even George W. Bush—who in many ways was successful in avoiding his father's judicial mistakes—wanted to replace Justice O'Connor with his longtime lawyer, Harriet Miers. Miers was a blank slate; her only known qualification was loyalty to the president. There was also President Bush's long-rumored desire to advance his other lawyer, Alberto Gonzales, to the Court. What did they think about the Constitution? Who knows! They're loyal, though, we were told at the time, so they'll be good.

Donald Trump, by virtue of being a businessman, didn't have these kinds of political hangers-on to push cronyism over conservatism. Moreover, it is not altogether clear that a run-of-the-mill Republican president would have stood so strongly for Brett Kavanaugh during his hellish ordeal. Any other Republican president would have been surrounded by establishment Republican aides who had an immediate need to be liked by the Georgetown and Kalorama set. So, when Christine Blasey Ford burst upon the scene, they might have advocated a swift retreat.

Indeed, we saw it happen: no federal judge was better connected among the bipartisan legal establishment than Brett Kavanaugh, and yet all of those carefully cultivated friends ran for the hills when Ford showed up. Even a few of his own law clerks stabbed him in the back. Not Trump. He had received the same treatment from his former friends on the left, and he knew exactly what to do. Show the Left how they do it in Queens: unleash Kavanaugh, fight back hard.

Trump understood the importance of conservative judges. He therefore empowered his—largely Catholic—staff to prioritize the finding of solid textualists and originalists above all else, preferably with proven track records who were also young. In large part he did this by recognizing the adage that personnel is policy and out-sourcing judicial selection to his White House counsels, Don McGahn and Pat Cipollone.

McGahn, a former student of the great pro-lifer Fr. Wilson Miscamble of Notre Dame, relentlessly sought the best-qualified, youngest originalist nominees he could find. This practice was continued by the conservative Catholic Cipollone and his conservative Catholic deputy Kate Todd. The controversial nominees were guided through their unusually brutal confirmation processes by still another conservative Catholic in Beth Williams, the head of the DOJ's Office of Legal Policy.

It also bears noting that Trump has been able to achieve his judicial goals thanks to the support of the U.S. Senate. In previous eras, Senate leadership would have seen judges as just another log to be rolled, a chit to be cashed for something important, like pork-barrel spending. Luckily President Trump has been working in partnership with Majority Leader Mitch McConnell, who uniquely among Republican leaders understands the incomparable importance of the courts and therefore famously ground judicial nominations to a halt for Obama's final two years, even going so far as to look Obama in the eyes and tell him that he would not fill the late Justice Scalia's seat.

Trump has also had stalwart allies in Chairmen Grassley and Graham of the Judiciary Committee. Gone are the days of liberal

Chairman Arlen Specter grilling John Roberts and Samuel Alito on whether or not *Roe v. Wade* is "super-duper precedent." Instead Chairmen Grassley and Graham have relentlessly processed Trump's nominees through the Judiciary Committee to help McConnell confirm record numbers of judges.

In one of the great team efforts of this administration, President Trump, his staff, Leader McConnell, and Chairmen Grassley and Graham have all had the same goal: get judges confirmed and watch them enforce the law and interpret the Constitution as written.

Which brings us to the details of Trump's court picks. Donald Trump is changing the face of the federal judiciary, and Catholics should care deeply about this. Perhaps the number one reason for Catholics to support Donald Trump for another presidential term is what he has done and promises to do in the federal courts, most especially the Supreme Court but also the inferior federal courts. This is of supreme importance and, as we said earlier, is the way the president may most firmly put his stamp on policy and even culture.

First, some raw numbers that terrify the Left.

Trump's changes to the Supreme Court are already well-known. By installing Justices Gorsuch and Kavanaugh, he has likely established a durable conservative majority on the Court. Far less well-known is his work on the circuit courts of appeals.

The federal courts are divided by three levels: the Supreme Court, the courts of appeal, and the district courts. Cases go to trial at the district court and are then taken to the court of appeals. For most cases, that's where it stops, but for fewer than one hundred cases a year, the Supreme Court may choose to hear the case. The Supreme Court will typically only hear a case if it's a matter of exceptional importance or to resolve a split among the courts of appeals. This is why the courts of appeals are so important.

In the federal system, the courts of appeals are divided into circuits, thirteen altogether. When Trump took over, eight of them were dominated by Democrat appointees. Three had slim conservative majorities that likely would have flipped had Hillary Clinton been elected. Only a single circuit court was reliably conservative.

After four years of remarkable judicial picks, seven of thirteen circuit courts have durable conservative majorities—that is, they are populated by young conservatives who will serve for years. And as I said before, even the most radical circuit court, the Ninth out of San Francisco and covering most of the West, now boasts more than 30 percent conservative judges.

How have these new conservative judges done on the law?

Consider how they have dealt with the growing problem of "transgender" inmates.

One such case revolves around a man named Norman Varner, who, in 2012, was sentenced to fifteen years in federal prison and fifteen years of supervised release for child porn. In 2018, he told the court he had become a woman and wanted his prison identification to reflect that. Almost certainly, he wanted to eventually be sent to a woman's prison. Now, you can easily see that a Democrat-appointed court would agree with this gender insanity. But a three-judge panel that included Catholic Trump appointee Kyle Duncan said no. In his decision, Duncan practically mocked the idea of sixty-seven genders. He said employing such pronouns as "fae, faer, faers, faerself," ze (pronounced "zee"), and hir (pronounced "hear"), would hinder communications among the parties and, presumably, "would be enforceable through contempt powers."

Judge Duncan is not the only Trump-appointed judge to encounter "trans" prisoner issues. One of his colleagues on the Fifth Circuit, fellow Trump appointee Judge James Ho, had previously ruled, "A state does not inflict cruel and unusual punishment by declining to provide sex reassignment surgery to a transgender inmate."

Yet another Trump appointee, Judge Michael Scudder, joined Trump Supreme Court short-lister Judge Diane Sykes when she denied a gender-dysphoric inmate's suit for damages against Wisconsin prison officials for failing to provide gender surgery. Are you noticing a pattern?

But this is not nearly the only piece of good news to result from Trump's appointments. President Trump's judges have also made their impact on the right to life and on religious freedom in dozens of cases that have advanced these causes.

Trump has a truly astounding record that is getting better every day. He has already put his stamp on the federal judiciary in a way that will rival any president in history. And if Trump wins in 2020, it is highly likely that even ancient Ruth Bader Ginsburg (born in

1933) will throw in the towel and Trump will get yet another Supreme Court pick. Heck, with Stephen Breyer turning the corner around eighty (he was born in 1938), he might even get more.

These continuing changes are essential for issues like the right to life and religious liberty. If for no other reason, faithful Catholics must give their vote to Trump to allow him to complete this reform of the courts.

CHAPTER FIVE

Trump and LGBT

G ay rights is an area where some faithful Catholics will be disappointed in Trump. At the same time he was making his journey on the life issue, he was decidedly not making any kind of journey on the LGBT agenda. Like George Bush and the life issues, Trump was surrounded by family members who are friendly to the LGBT cause. There is no way Ivanka Trump does not favor the whole panoply of LGBT issues. Jared Kushner, too, and probably all the rest, including Melania.

Like his initial acceptance of abortion, his response on homosexual marriage was that he grew up in New York City. He said that to justify his acceptance of the LGBT agenda.

While the rainbow movement is not as vast as its members claim, it is very powerful. Gay activists say they are everywhere, but are they really? How could a group smaller than the Methodists be everywhere? The overall group of homosexuals in America maxes out at roughly 1.6 percent, according to the most robust data from the National Health Institute of the Center for Disease Control. Rainbow radicals began pushing the 10 percent figure back in the Jimmy Carter days. Small as it may be, the group is immensely powerful. Gays have come to dominate the levers of power in most major cultural centers, including Hollywood, the media, and even corporate C-suites. The annual ranking of gay-friendly companies produced by the anti-Christian Human Rights Campaign puts practically every major company in the country in the 100 percent gay-friendly category. Talk about pushing on an open door.

In what seemed like only a few years, this small but powerful group has turned the entire U.S. government around. Even the president of the United States, Barack Obama, moved from claiming he was against gay marriage—although this was very clearly a political tactic—to becoming a very vocal supporter of overturning American marriage laws. Although activists in support of man–woman marriage had won thirty-one statewide races, gay marriage supporters managed to get the courts to go along with them, culminating in the Supreme Court imposing same-sex marriage on the whole country.

According to gays who keep score on these things, Trump has a history of supportive words regarding homosexuality. In 1999, he said he supported gays openly serving in the military. He told *The Advocate* in 2000 that he agreed with amending the Civil Rights Act of 1964 to include sexual orientation. And in 2005 he congratulated Elton John on his marriage to another man. As recently as 2015, he said then-governor Pence had done "a bad job" in the battle between nondiscrimination against gays and religious freedom for Christians who did not want to bake the wedding cake. Trump even said that Caitlyn Jenner (formerly Bruce) could use any bathroom he wanted in Trump Tower.

In July 2016, I went along with hundreds of other faith leaders to a come-to-Trump meeting at a Times Square hotel. He repeatedly dodged LGBT questions. Though he offered strong support for other items on the religious Right's laundry list, he punted when it came to gay rights. "He might be coming our way on life," we thought, "but he's not doing a thing about the rainbow advance."

Now, there is great confusion about Church teaching on this issue. We have renegade priests like Fr. James Martin gallivanting around the country telling gays that Church teaching is too harsh, that it ought to change and very well could change, especially under this pope.

The Church teaches that while homosexuality is not intrinsically sinful, it is a disorder, and the catechism hints strongly at a psychological disorder, which is the traditional medical/scientific view. The Church teaches that homosexual acts are objectively sinful, even evil. The Church also teaches, however, that homosexuals should not suffer from "unjust" discrimination. Note that word "unjust." It means there are forms of just discrimination according to Church teaching. For instance, the Church teaches that gay adoption is immoral and does "violence" to the child. For instance, men and women who flaunt their disordered sexual inclinations are fired from jobs with the Church on account of giving scandal to the faithful. People like Fr. James Martin squawk that the Church is not so quick to fire those using contraception, IVF, and other things equally sinful. The answer is that these sins are not quite so public as two men getting married, which is where they usually run into trouble with a local parish.

There is the problem with the pope, who seems interested in making some sort of inchoate changes. His famous "Who am I to judge?" quip, made on a plane to a journalist, has been very durable in carrying supposed change upon the air. Some hold that this random comment has changed Church teaching on homosexuality. Francis was actually commenting on a priest who may have had such inclinations but who was trying to live in accordance with Church teaching. This is still not good. After all, the inclination is itself a signal of deeper problems, though there is a movement among some young people who are homosexually inclined and argue that one can be out and about as a homosexual just as long as one does not act upon the desire. I call this movement the New Homophiles. They are a problematic group, but their view is far better than Fr. James Martin's attitude of throw the doors open and let the unrepentant Rainbows in.

In the light of obvious changes in elite opinion—not necessarily changes in the opinion of regular people; it is hardly a moment of celebration when a father and mother hear their son wants to be sexual with other men—what is Trump do to?

Turns out he made the elite gays quite upset. In fact, no matter what he might do for them, and he has done much, they really don't like him. And he has acted more in accordance with Church teaching than practically anyone would have thought.

One of the first things he did was reverse course on transgender bathrooms in public schools. Recall that Obama's Department of Education sent a letter to all school districts telling them they must allow gender-confused kids to use the bathroom they identify with. This would put boys in girls' bathrooms, showers, and hotel rooms on overnight field trips. It should be understood that this was not an order from the federal government; it was a guidance letter from a mid-level flunky at the Department of Education that was nonetheless taken as gospel by certain liberal school boards.

However, things changed when, within a few days of his inauguration, Trump rescinded the guidance letter, the Supreme Court bounced the letter, and the case crumbled, at least for now.

Be that as it may, Trump continues to be a mixed and sometimes confusing bag. In 2019, President Trump tweeted support for so-called "Pride Month," when the Western world is festooned with rainbow imagery and gaudy sexualized parades surge down the streets of American and European cities. This was the first time Trump had acknowledged the month-long celebration.

While Trump may have personally acknowledged "Pride Month," he put a stop to the gross identification of the American flag around the world with the gay agenda. Under President Obama, U.S. embassies across the globe were ordered to fly the rainbow flag alongside the flag of the United States. Ambassadors took to marching in so-called "Pride parades." They took to inviting local homosexual communities into the embassy for gay-themed parties, even in Muslim countries where this insulted the host country.

During "Pride Month" 2019, word went out from the Trump State Department that the rainbow flag could not fly with the American flag. While most embassies complied, some, such as the U.S. Mission to the United Nations, tried to come up with ways to get around the new rule. In a sign of blatant disrespect to the chain of command, these embassies fixed the rainbow flag to nearby elevated poles. But at least the local populace knew that this was in direct conflict with the expressed preference of the American people.

Yet each step forward has come with at least one step back. While fighting the official celebration of homosexuality in American embassies, the Trump White House has allowed his ambassador to Germany to begin a global campaign to pressure countries to strike down laws against homosexual behavior, something that was also against the law here until it was overturned by the Supreme Court in the *Lawrence v. Texas* decision, a decision Justice Antonin Scalia correctly said would lead inexorably to same-sex marriage. The U.S. effort, led by Ambassador Richard Grenell, who is homosexual and has marched in the German "Pride parade," was said to be aimed only at countries where the death penalty was administered for certain egregious sexual acts, e.g., raping an underage boy or deliberately infecting someone with

HIV/AIDs. However, Grenell cast a much wider net than that. He targeted more than seventy countries where there were any laws regulating homosexual behavior.

Another step back occurred in a little-known process at the UN in Geneva called the Universal Periodic Review, in which governments are invited to criticize each other on human rights issues. Criticism is supposed to focus on existing categories of human rights, ones that are recognized under the various human rights treaties generally agreed to. Under President Obama, the United States began pressuring countries on "non-discrimination" based on sexual orientation and gender identity (SOGI). According to leftist ideologues, SOGI should be placed on par with established human rights like freedom of religion and freedom of the press. The United States does not even recognize non-discrimination based on SOGI in domestic law, let alone in international human rights law. Yet, here were our diplomats demanding that foreign governments accept legal standards that we don't recognize here. Sadly, the initiative-started by the Obama administration was continued under the Trump State Department. It is still going on as of this writing. Does this gain any support from gay elites? Not one bit.

Trump failed to overturn some other controversial Obama administration policies. For instance, the Obama administration issued a very troubling guidance memo to be used in the implementation and administration of U.S. grants overseas through the U.S. Agency for International Development (USAID). A high-ranking official at USAID, a Trump appointee, tells me that gays occupy many of the top spots at the agency and insist their issue takes top priority. With the help of their allies in Congress and a White House reluctant to fight on this issue, they ensured the guidance was not changed when Trump came in. The guidance not only identifies restrictive abortion laws as obstacles to women's equality, it further requires organizations to use funding and programming meant for women and direct it to men who identify as homosexual or transgender.

At the end of 2018, Ivanka Trump played a key role in the passage of something called the Women's Entrepreneurship and Economic Empowerment Act, which aims to help women expand small and medium-sized businesses in foreign countries. While that may sound like a laudable initiative, the law included language first drafted in the Obama era, using what may sound like an appealing law to smuggle a radical ideological project into American foreign policy. Social conservatives fought very hard to exclude the Obama-era gender guidance in the new law, but they failed.

To be sure, Trump is not to be blamed fully for these developments at the international level. The career staff of the federal government in all the agencies has been flooded with homosexual advocates and activists. One friend at the State Department told me that no meeting on any subject fails to include some aspect of the homosexual question. Given the lay of the land, it is very hard to change the narrative and the policies attendant to that movement. Moreover, it takes a remarkable amount of courage to stand up to activist bureaucrats because they have the power to destroy careers and reputations. Gays are nothing if not the masters of ruining someone's life over petty policy differences.

Domestically, one would think the LGBT movement had gotten everything it wanted before Trump. Gays can marry. Gays can adopt. Gays have become a favored group in the law and, even more importantly, among America's rich and powerful. There is nary an American corporation that has not bought into the LGBT agenda. In fact, those who may oppose the LGBT advance are the ones who can lose their jobs and be chased out of polite society. Even so, the LGBTs are pushing very hard for something called the Equality Act, which would penalize everyday Americans for their beliefs about marriage and human sexuality.

The proposal, which passed the United States House of Representatives in May 2019, would amend the 1964 Civil Rights Act to "prohibit discrimination on the basis of sex, sexual orientation, gender identity, or pregnancy, childbirth, or a related medical condition of an individual, as well as because of sex-based stereotypes." The new Equality Act could very well lead to quotas for the gender-confused and certainly for homosexuals. As we discussed in the chapter on religious freedom, this is already happening, with the most obvious example being Colorado baker Jack Phillips, who refused to bake a wedding cake for a gay ceremony.

A Heritage Foundation briefing paper on the Equality Act tells the story of Peter Vlaming, a French teacher who was dismissed under his school's antidiscrimination policy when he refused to use a female student's preferred masculine pronouns. According to the report, "Vlaming had tried to accommodate the student by avoiding pronouns altogether and addressing the student by her preferred masculine name, but this was deemed insufficient by the school board."

Heritage also claims that Catholic hospitals in California and New Jersey have been sued for declining to perform hysterectomies on otherwise healthy women who want to become men. One Catholic hospital in Washington was sued by the ACLU for refusing to cut off the breasts of a gender dysphoric sixteen-year-old girl. The case was eventually settled out of court.

Here, we find a compelling argument for supporting Donald Trump. While President Trump may be a mixed bag when it comes to gay rights, the current fight has moved past the question of homosexuality. Today, the Right has to destroy a radical gender ideology that threatens to upend the basis of human life as we know it.

Radical feminists, who have become allies of social conservatives on the transgender issue, argue that the Equality Act would continue what they call the erasure of women. The Heritage brief tells the story of "Pascha Thomas [who] was forced to remove her child from school after a male classmate assaulted her five-year-old daughter in the girls' restroom. The boy had access to the girls' restroom because of the school's policy that grants students access to private facilities on the basis of self-identified gender identity."

There are dozens more examples of the intrusion of gender ideology into the private sphere. And it could get much worse. The Equality Act would make all of this a matter not just of federal law, but of federal civil rights law, which is hallowed, even sacred ground, never to be questioned under threat of reputational ruin.

The gay activists have moved on to another battle in the culture war. Marriage is already out of style for the activists. Now, they want to force gender ideology down America's throat. On that issue, Trump has acted more in accordance with Church teaching than anyone would have thought.

Even Pope Francis, hardly the most willing fighter in the culture wars, has condemned "gender ideology" and the idea we can technologically alter our sex. In July 2016, Pope Francis said, "In Europe, America, Latin America, Africa, and in some countries of Asia, there are genuine forms of ideological colonization taking place. And one of these—I will call it clearly by its name—is [the ideology of] 'gender.' Today children—children!—are taught in school that everyone can choose his or her sex. Why are they teaching this? Because the books are provided by the persons and institutions that give you money. These forms of ideological colonization are also supported by influential countries. And this is terrible!"

Francis continued with even stronger language: "In a conversation with Pope Benedict, who is in good health and very perceptive, he said to me: 'Holiness, this is the age of sin against God the Creator.' He is very perceptive. God created man and woman; God created the world in a certain way...and we are doing the exact opposite. God gave us things in a 'raw' state, so that we could shape a culture; and then with this culture, we are shaping things that bring us back to the 'raw' state! Pope Benedict's observation should make us think. 'This is the age of sin against God the Creator.' That will help us."

So far, Trump has resisted the call for this massive federal intrusion into how Catholics live their private and professional lives. When the Equality Act was passed out of the U.S. House in May 2019, a Trump spokesman said the act would "effectively nullify the Religious Freedom Restoration Act," which is absolutely true. Chad Griffin, head of the often anti-Christian Human Rights Campaign, said he was "disgusted but not surprised."

They were also upset when his political appointees at the Department of Health and Human Services derailed a last-minute rule change by President Obama that prohibited discrimination based on "sexual orientation and gender identity." Trump's people changed that to "to the extent doing so is prohibited by federal statutes." Since "sexual orientation and gender identity" is not part of the 1964 Civil Rights Act and since the Equality Act has not passed, this was scuttled for the time being. Attorneys general in seventeen states and the District of Columbia have filed suit.

Trump appointees also removed anti-discrimination language in the U.S. Department of the Interior, citing the fact that sexual orientation and gender identity are not protected categories under the 1964 law.

Trump also rejected the notion that the gender-confused could serve in the United States military. Only a few years after the door was opened for out-and-proud gays to serve in the military came pressure to allow men who pose as women and women who pose as men to serve. There was even a proposal for U.S. taxpayers to pay for the "sex change" operations of serving members of the military. Imagine taxpayer money going to pay for cutting off otherwise healthy tissue like breasts and penises or for drugs to inhibit testosterone or estrogen. The proposition also placed men who think they are women into the sleeping quarters and showers of real women. Women who complained would be punished. Trump cancelled all of that.

It should be noted that the Church does not teach there is such a thing as a sex change or that same-sex attraction is inborn or immutable. The Church still teaches that genital activity between people of the same sex is mortally sinful, objectively evil. The Church also teaches there is such a thing as "just discrimination" when it comes to homosexuals. So, there is nothing in the actions or beliefs of President Trump and his administration that would come into conflict with Church teaching. In fact, his actions comport more closely with Church teaching on this issue than any of the candidates of the Democratic Party.

Without a doubt, President Trump has a great deal of sympathy for those who are same-sex attracted. During the campaign he held up a sign saying LGBTs for Trump. He is proud of their support. His ambassador to Germany may be an out homosexual and a global campaigner for gay rights, but Trump still draws a line at the imposition of the gay and transgender ideology upon the American people and our institutions, and that is as good a reason to support President Trump as any.

On the other hand, the entire Democratic Party seems to stand in opposition to Church teaching when it comes to homosexuality and transgenderism. The Democratic Party has become a wholly owned subsidiary of the LGBT movement. To stand in opposition to it is career suicide for any Democrat. They are also backed by the muscle and might of America's corporations large and small. In 2020, the Human Rights Campaign's annual survey of "equality" was presented at the prestigious Davos World Economic Forum. That survey found that nearly 100 percent of the Fortune 500 have a 100 percent rating, meaning that Christian belief and practice are not welcome in the halls and factories of American big business.

When evaluating Trump's stance on LGBT issues, Catholics must take the current state of play into consideration. The private sector, along with the Democratic Party, is the LGBT movement's most vocal advocate. Political appointees who stand firm against the LGBT elite will be targeted in their later lives. They will be inhibited from getting jobs in corporate America. Their resolve and bravery, including Trump's, should be recognized by faithful Catholics.

While it may not be President Trump's central issue, he is clearly fighting to defend Americans from the ever encroaching gender ideology advanced by leftist advocates. Their legislative agenda would abolish religious liberty as we know it, both at home and abroad.

CHAPTER SIX

Trump and Immigration

In January 2020, it was reported that President Trump was going to impose "visa restrictions on pregnant women." At first blush, this seemed like some kind of crazy, vicious, and even misogynistic and racist program. The announcement fit perfectly into the existing narrative that Trump hates women and is certainly not pro-life. How could this monster deny pregnant women entry into the United States?

In reality, Trump wasn't fighting pregnancy. He was taking a crack at what's known as "birth tourism," whereby pregnant women travel to the United States in the days before the expected birth so that their child can be born on U.S. soil and get a coveted U.S. passport. This is so-called "birthright" citizenship, whereby anyone born on U.S. soil can legally claim U.S. citizenship. Such citizenship is a constitutional right. But it produces what some call an "anchor" baby from whom whole families can legally immigrate to the United States. Thousands from around the world game the system every year, going straight from the customs line at an American airport to the neonatal ward.

Apparently "birth tourism" is a big business both here and overseas. According to the Associated Press, "American companies take out advertisements and charge up to $80,000 to facilitate the practice, offering hotel rooms and medical care." Many pregnant women have traveled from Russia and China to give birth on U.S. soil.

Of course, it is nearly impossible to discern the intention of arriving women. And the practice is legal. Birth tourism companies are sometimes prosecuted for visa fraud or tax evasion. But the women are often up-front about what they are doing, producing signed contracts with doctors and hospitals.

Trump issued a new rule based on national security that any woman suspected of coming for birth purposes only can be denied a visa. The conservative Center for Immigration Studies estimated in 2012 that upwards of thirty-six thousand foreign women gave birth in the United States and then left. Just to emphasize: the child is then considered an American citizen and can come back anytime. Under U.S. law the child's family may come, too. Often, extended families claim immigration status based on that one birth.

The Left, and most especially the Catholic Left, firmly believes its trump card against Donald Trump is immigration. You will hear incessantly about splitting up families, children in cages, and hunting down illegal aliens. Plus, it is now forbidden to call them "illegal"; they are merely "undocumented." You will hear about Trump's racist intent with regard to immigration and his supposed dog-whistling to white supremacists, white nationalists, and other unsavory boogeymen of left-wing nightmares.

Without a doubt, this is an area where the Left and the Catholic Left may be getting the most traction. On the one hand, most Americans are suspicious of illegal aliens. We think, quite correctly, that it is not entirely fair for people to sneak across our border in order to jump the line in front of people who have waited patiently, often for years, to become legal immigrants to this country. On the other hand, Americans firmly believe we are a nation of immigrants, and this is largely true. And so, it seems especially heartless that Trump and his followers would want to stem the tide of people who seem to be just like us and our ancestors, yearning to breathe free.

This is a sticky issue for Catholics because the pope and the bishops seem to have come down so strongly on behalf of both illegal aliens and those who claim refugee status, no matter how questionable the claim. Members of the Holy See have openly advocated on behalf of those who come in large caravans from Central America to our southern border. Recall that in his only visit to the United States, Pope Francis celebrated Mass along the Mexican border. This was a boon to the open borders crowd and a stick in the eye to Donald Trump, who has pledged to build a wall to keep illegals at bay. The pope also said it is not Christian to build walls, failing to point out that the Vatican has very high walls with guards at each entrance to Vatican City who keep out anyone and everyone not on the approved list to enter. And yes, St. Peter's is on Vatican property and anyone can go there, but no one can get past it to the other side and the warren of charming streets, old buildings, luscious gardens, and Vatican offices. Entry is as verboten as any crossing from Juarez to El Paso. In fact, it would be harder to sneak through St. Anne's Gate into the Vatican City State than it is to wade across the Rio Grande into El Paso.

It is important to take a close look at what the Church actually teaches about immigration, and there are voluminous documents and statements available. The Church does not teach open borders, even remotely. We are not required to believe that anyone who comes to our border must be allowed to come in. No matter what the Catholic Left says, this is simply false propaganda.

Church teaching on immigration seems contradictory, so much so that one tony conservative Frenchman wondered, "I don't know what I am supposed to believe about immigration." He wrote, "I do not know what I believe. I do not know what I believe because my heart breaks for those who are, or feel, forced to leave their land, who want to make a better life, who suffer." One notes immediately the high-level emotion that not so much creeps into the immigration debate but is part and parcel of it. The emotionalism runs high, which is one of the reasons open borders propaganda features so-called "Dreamers," kids inevitably getting straight A's or working hard for a better life. Wouldn't it be awful if they or their parents were deported when their only crime was sneaking across a border decades ago?

The emoting is about the hard cases, the people who have broken our laws, come across the border without permission, and may have set up shop here for years. There is a great deal of unloading also about those who style themselves refugees, fleeing from what they claim is violence in their own countries. I will talk about this later in the chapter, but this country is among the most generous in the world for accepting foreign nationals on our shores legally and offering them a chance of actually becoming citizens. Many countries allow immigrants into their countries, but they are never allowed actually to become Saudis, for instance; they are only ever noncitizen foreign workers. There is also the problem of acceptance. The great Jewish legal scholar Joseph Weiler from New York University School of Law lectured in Vienna many years ago and said that immigrants to France, for instance, even ones who become citizens, will never be considered French, whereas a legal immigrant to the United States who becomes a citizen is always considered a citizen and not a foreigner.

So, what does the Church teach? The Church teaches the right of individuals and families to seek better lives in other countries. This is the same reason that my ancestor left England and came to the colonies in 1740 to seek a better life, perhaps a more exciting life, one that he got when the revolution came and he fought in George Washington's army. So, we understand in our American bones that we welcome immigrants. Our beliefs are not in opposition to the Church teaching that we must welcome the stranger. But we are also not required by Holy Mother Church to accept anyone and everyone who knocks on our door. The Church teaches sovereign borders that allow governments to regulate who may come in. The Church also recognizes the right of governments to determine who is and who is not a citizen.

It is unfortunate that the U.S. Conference of Catholic Bishops issued a document called "Welcoming the Stranger among Us: Unity in Diversity" that made the issue more confused for Catholics. The document characterizes immigration critics as nativists, ethno-centrists, and racists. The document says such notions have become "popular in different parts of our country." The document focuses largely on immigrants who come to the country in "desperate circumstances," as if these are the only circumstances in which people would want to come to the United States. Most people want to come to the United States because they believe in the American dream. They are not so much running from gangs and marauding armies as they are running into the arms of the amazing opportunities afforded not just the native-born and naturalized citizens but also immigrants who can see their dreams come true. The Left, and I include the Catholic bishops here, cast the immigration debate as a great tragedy for people who have to leave their countries to come to the land of milk and honey.

There are plenty of biblical citations encouraging populations to welcome immigrants and even refugees. Abraham moved to

Egypt, as did the Holy Family when they were under threat from Herod. Pope Pius XII referred to the Holy Family as "the archetype of every refugee family." Abraham's wife Sarah "extended bounteous hospitality" to three strangers who were a manifestation of the Lord. Jesus said in Matthew, "For I was hungry, and you gave me food, I was thirsty, and you gave me drink, a stranger and you welcomed me."

What is striking about the document from the bishop's conference, however, is how quickly it dismisses the concerns of everyday Americans. "The treatment of the immigrant too often reflects failures of understanding and sinful patterns of chauvinism, prejudice, and discrimination," the conference writes. They forget the fact that Americans are among the most generous in the world with regard to immigration. The bishops cite nativism and how Americans have forgotten our "immigrant" past. They bang the drum for "multiculturalism," which has become so harmful to our country as it has become a weapon in the hands of the hard Left. It is really a rather shocking document.

It should be pointed out that the conferences of bishops that produce these documents are institutions that Cardinal Ratzinger insisted have no role in the hierarchy of the Church. The regular Catholic plugs into the Church though his own bishop and, through him, the pope. National bishops' conferences can set certain norms of worship and give advice, even policy advice, but Catholics are free to practice their own prudential judgment about what it means to "welcome the stranger" and much else. So, one may in good faith disregard conference documents on immigration, no matter how many times the Catholic Left cites them.

A follow-up document in 2003 was no less negative, asserting that our European ancestors "came to conquer and colonize these lands, displacing and eliminating entire peoples." The 2003 document cites five principles on immigration: 1) Persons have the right to find opportunities in their homeland, 2) Persons have a right to migrate to support themselves and their families, 3) Sovereign states have the right to control their borders (but within limits), 4) Refugees and asylum seekers should be afforded protection, and 5) The human dignity and human rights of undocumented migrants should be respected.

The reality faced by Americans all across the country, and most especially along the border with Mexico, is a sense of being overwhelmed and of social services systems being bogged down, sometimes completely. The bishops seem to believe that our country can absorb massive numbers of legal and illegal immigrants and that the impact should be no concern of ours. In fact, much like the liberal Left, they seem to believe that such a concern itself is a form of racism and xenophobia.

But since when is it racist to express concerns about the collapse in social services caused by mass illegal immigration? These problems affect people of all races, including native-born Hispanics and African Americans. It should be noted that the U.S. Conference of Catholic Bishops receives millions of dollars—$91 million in 2016 alone—for work on the refugee issue. Catholic Charities received $200 million. One Catholic organization in Boston got $17 million. This is not to say the bishops and Catholic charities are motivated by money. But with millions paid out for sexual abuse victims and drops in contributions from regular pew sitters, the money is an important factor.

This is not to say there is not much to admire in Mexican immigrants, even those who come across the border illegally. Imagine the tenacity they have to brave those long and dangerous crossings. They put me in mind of my own ancestors who got on leaky boats and braved several months crossing to North America. But Americans did not agree to these wholesale changes in the American culture. It should be noted that encouraging assimilation is now considered racism. Those old enough will remember households of recent legal immigrants who spoke the old language at home but whose children were eager to become American, to inherit all the culture of the typical American teen. Immigrant parents, too, might have wanted their children to retain some of the old ways, to respect their foreign heritage, but they wanted their children to become American as soon as possible. It can be seen how people all over the world, especially young people, seek to emulate our American ways, for both good and bad.

Here in the States, one sees an increasing rejection of American culture and ideals and an attempt to reject assimilation and refuse to blend in to the dominant culture. Millions of Americans see an America that no longer resembles what they grew up with. This is something even the Catholic bishops are not prepared to address because it seems xenophobic and contrary to the new gospel of "multiculturalism" that is really a kind of code to reject American ideals and, more relevant to the Catholic Church, Western Civilization itself.

The current issue animating the political debate in America is not primarily the legal immigration of people who wait for years to gain legal admittance and citizenship. Rather, it is illegal immigrants who seek to jump the line in front of all those others who are patiently waiting. It is also those claiming persecution in their home country. Trump wants to bring illegal immigration to an end, rightfully claiming that a nation that cannot control its borders can hardly be called a nation at all.

The complex nature of the immigration debate lends itself to simplistic and emotional slogans. We are led to think of the kids in cages rather than the nuances of policy. There is almost nothing quite so emotionally charged as the image of kids locked in cages, or the "concentration camps" as some have described them.

Not that long ago, most illegals crossing the border were single adult men. In 2014, during the Obama administration, things changed dramatically. Children, often unaccompanied, started flooding the border, causing a massive crisis. This abated somewhat during Trump's first year in office because word got out that it would be much harder to pass through the process and simply disappear into America's cities.

The reality is that the U.S. government, even under President Trump, cares deeply about these unaccompanied children, who were put at risk by being placed with predatory smugglers to cross hundreds and even thousands of miles of dangerous territory and attempt entry into the American promised land.

A child who is apprehended at the border may spend a few days in a "cage," that is, a safe and secure chain-link enclosure. Then he is placed in the care of the Department of Health and Human Services, which is required by law to provide care for all children until they are released to a suitable sponsor, parent, or close relative. These children may be released from HHS care if they return to their home country, turn eighteen, or gain legal immigrant status.

What about family separation? This is a sticky question. Children have been separated from their mothers and fathers because their parents are considered in violation of the law when they come across the border without permission and therefore must be remanded for the adjudication of their cases. Nowhere in our criminal justice system are children housed with their arrested fathers and mothers, as that would also expose them to other adults.

It very well could be that these adults will gain access to the country because they credibly claim persecution back home. Overwhelmingly, these claims are judged not credible and are denied. But even when the claims are accepted as possibly true, only a small percentage of the immigrants arrange for asylum. Most of them simply disappear, thanks to the practice known as "catch and release."

Immigration is a very complicated issue, filled with as much legal nuance as any federal policy debate. But instead of providing the facts, the Left tries to demonize all efforts to enforce a sensible immigration policy. Leftists want to open the borders and let everyone come in. They may deny it, but it is hard to see any other way to solve the problem that would be sufficient or fair or "Catholic" for them.

Let me close this chapter with two considerations.

First, there is a great deal of dishonesty in the immigration debate. If you oppose illegal immigration, you are charged with opposing "immigration." Distinctions mean nothing to the Left because making the distinction would take away the heat of their arguments. It should be noted that President Trump does not propose to change the remarkably generous U.S. policy for legal immigration. Trump loves legal immigrants. He has married two of them!

Second, I will discuss something the bishops and other advocates seem reticent to discuss: the economic impact of illegal immigration on our country and on lower-skilled American workers. It should be noted that among the great champions for low-skilled workers are the Chamber of Commerce and major corporations.

I will deal with the second proposition first: the economic impact of immigration, both legal and illegal.

Some argue that illegal immigration is an unmitigated plus, even a boon to the economy. It should be remembered that no less a leftist Catholic hero than Cesar Chavez, founder of the United

Farm Workers, vehemently opposed illegal immigration. As illegal immigration opponent Mark Krikorian wrote, "[Chavez's] views on border control would be a perfect fit in the Trump administration." Chavez opposed the "bracero program" that legally imported cheap labor from Mexico. He protested illegal immigration at the Mexican border, where he was joined by the Reverend Ralph Abernathy and Senator Walter Mondale, both liberals. Chavez even ran a border patrol program called the "wet line." Using a phrase like the "wet line" would get you run out of polite society these days.

What the Left knew then was that cheap illegal labor from south of the border had a very harmful effect on native agricultural workers, many of whom were of Hispanic origin themselves. What changed is that the Left needed a new raft of voters and big business needed more cheap labor. In fact, besides the Democratic Party, the biggest cheerleader for illegal immigration in America is big business, most especially food processing and the service industries.

Consider the case of Crider, Inc., a chicken processing plant that was raided by immigration agents in May 2007. Fully 75 percent of its largely Hispanic and obviously illegal workforce simply disappeared. According to scholar George Borjas, "Shortly after, Crider placed an ad in the local newspaper announcing job openings at higher wages."

Borjas came to national attention when Trump accepted the GOP nomination in July 2016. Borjas has studied the impact of illegal and legal immigration on the American economy and on native employees. He concluded that those hit hardest financially by low-skilled immigration were low-skilled native employees, especially those in the black and Hispanic communities. He argues there is a $50 billion boon to the economy because of immigrants entering our economy, but that this is offset by roughly the same amount that is doled out to immigrants on public assistance. He says the great beneficiary of low-skilled immigration is the business community, precisely the complaint of leftist Cesar Chavez decades ago.

The Left wants us to believe that America is among the stingiest countries in the world when it comes to immigration. This is utterly false. According to UN figures, more than 46 million foreign-born nationals currently live in the United States. Want to know the nearest country to us? Germany, with 12 million. After that, Russia with 11 million. The United Kingdom hosts 8.5 million. Spain has 6.3 million. The Netherlands, 1.9 million. What about supposedly friendly Demark? 572,000.

There is also no evidence that Donald Trump wants to change U.S. policy on legal immigration. He has not proposed that we change the total numbers or percentages of legal immigrants allowed into the United States from specific geographic areas. He has not proposed a legal immigration pause such as we had for much of the twentieth century so that the existing immigrants could assimilate into American culture. Trump has not proposed that we become something other than a "nation of immigrants."

The talking point most often used as a rapier against Trump is the biblical admonition that we "welcome the stranger." It is implied that Trump does not want to "welcome the stranger," and therefore voting for him is somehow a violation of Church teaching. However, there is no evidence whatsoever that Trump wants to turn away the stranger. He is concerned about issues related to illegal immigration, and, as the Church teaches, we may defend our national sovereignty and our borders. So, the Catholic Left's argument that supporting Donald Trump violates the Church's teaching on immigration is patently dishonest.

CHAPTER SEVEN

Trump and the Environment

Some, perhaps most, in the Catholic hierarchy are all in on catastrophic man-made climate change. You might say they believe it religiously. They believe it is going to happen. It is happening now and if we don't act immediately to eliminate all fossil fuel use, we are all doomed. DOOMED. No doomsday evangelical from previous centuries had anything on these guys. The world is going to end because of climate change.

Donald Trump may not be skeptical of a warming planet, but he is skeptical about the catastrophic nature of the claims and certainly skeptical about the elimination of fossil fuels. Does this mean Trump stands against Church teaching on the environment? Does this mean Catholics who support Trump are no more than "cafeteria Catholics" on the environment? Trump has done a tremendous amount to shock and anger the alarmists among us, including those in the Church. Trump has undone what appear to be dozens of environmental "advances" in the first few years of his first term.

But before we get to President Trump, we have to clarify the Church's teaching. We have to start with the pope and some of the bishops.

When it comes to the environment, the big megillah is the pope's hefty, 180-page encyclical *Laudato si'*, issued in May 2015, said to be prepared in advance of the final negotiating session of the Paris Climate Accord in December of that year. Catholic lefties say *Laudato si'* was an attempt by the pope to affect the outcome of the Paris Climate Accord that was to be finalized by the governments of the world. According to the Catholic lefties, anyone who does not believe that climate catastrophe is both real and man-made rejects the magisterial teachings of the Church. Moreover, this makes you "anti-Francis."

Laudato si' demonstrated where Francis stood, not in the argument between Left and Right but in the argument between, as Ross Douthat put it, "dynamists" and "catastrophists." Dynamists believe we can solve the problem simply by moving forward and letting mankind's mastery fix the problem. "Catastrophists" are, well, catastrophists, the-end-is-nigh folks. The pope is in the latter camp. The question is whether all Catholics are required to join the pope in catastrophism.

Pope Francis tells us, "There are regions now at high risk and, aside from all doomsday predictions, the present world system is certainly unsustainable from a number of points of view. . . ." He says, "Doomsday predictions can no longer be met with irony or disdain. We may well be leaving to coming generations debris, desolation and filth. The pace of consumption, waste and environmental change has so stretched the planet's capacity that our contemporary lifestyle, unsustainable as it is, can only precipitate catastrophes, such as those which even now periodically occur in different areas of the world."

Pope Francis calls for radical political change on account of his views on the climate. According to the Holy Father, "Humanity is called to recognize the need for changes of lifestyle, production and consumption in order to combat warming or at least the human causes which produce or aggravate it." He does admit there may be other factors such as volcanic activity, variations in the Earth's orbit, and the solar cycle. But he hangs his hat on what he calls "a number of" scientific studies indicating that most global warming in recent decades is due to carbon dioxide, methane, nitrogen oxides, and other gases related to human activity. To be sure, there are probably hundreds of scientific studies that say such things. Maybe they are right, maybe not.

While all this may be Pope Francis's belief, what is the level of magisterial teaching? Is it now against Church teaching to meet doomsday predictions with irony and disdain? Are the millions of Catholics who still meet such end-of-the-world scenarios with both irony and disdain now outside the Church? Lefty Catholics would say so. Lefty Catholics argue that if you disagree, if you go so far as believing "climate change" is a massive hoax, you commit sin by rejecting Church teaching. Are Catholics now required to believe in catastrophic man-made "climate change"? The Pope makes it abundantly clear that he believes in man-man climate catastrophe, but is that now a dogma of the faith?

The answer is no. Faithful Catholics are utterly free to reject the proposition that the globe is warming catastrophically due to mankind's patterns of consumption. Rejecting this notion does not put one outside the Church, no matter what the Catholic Left says about you or President Trump.

But *Laudato si'* goes even further. Must we as faithful Catholics agree with the Holy Father that there must be "the establishment of a legal framework which can set clear boundaries and ensure the protection of eco-systems"? Must we believe in the establishment of a global political body to monitor and regulate the global ecological commons? Is it an article of our faith that we must believe in the United Nations and the hideous documents produced there? Must we turn over our national sovereignty to a global authority? To be sure, at least since the time of John XXIII the Church has promoted a global authority and participated in various UN bodies, but must we agree? Must we agree with the Church in its multilateral diplomatic agreements?

It should be pointed out that the pope has invited some very sketchy people to advise him on these issues, including John Schellnhuber, a German atheist who said the United States needed to reduce our CO_2 emissions to—get this—zero by 2020. He is also known for arguing that the Earth's carrying capacity is no more than 1 billion people, which begs the question about what the pope's adviser would do with the excess 6 billion.

Lefty Catholics jumped into climate change with both feet. Well before *Laudato si'*, but given great encouragement by the document, massive coalitions were formed to fight global catastrophic man-made climate change. Perhaps the largest among them is the "Global Catholic Climate Movement," which claims nine hundred member organizations. This coalition gives you plenty to do. You can become a *Laudato si'* "animator," convene a *Laudato si'* "circle," or attend a *Laudato si'* "circuit." You can "green your parish." It sounds more like the flower generation than the Catholic Church.

There are working groups you can join, including one on "eco-spirituality" that even offers a *Laudato si'* hymnal. There is the working group on "eco-conversion" where you "collaborate with Catholic partners on the 'Seasons of Creation'" with prayer services, tree plantings, and webinars.

But what is a lefty campaign without calls for divestment of institutional funds? In June 2016, on the anniversary of *Laudato si'*, four religious orders announced they were divesting from fossil fuels. Four months later, seven more Catholic organizations announced their commitment to divest. This included "a major healthcare network with 24 hospitals, 300 doctors' offices, and 40,000 employees." By September 2019, the divestment effort claimed $11 trillion had been pulled out of the fossil fuel market.

To be sure, not all of this was Catholic money, but organizers claimed the largest single faith group involved in the campaign was the Catholic Church.

Among the statements announcing divestment was one from the Archdiocese of Ancona-Osimo, located on the Adriatic coast of Italy. The archdiocese claimed, quite remarkably, that they were joining the divestment campaign from fossil fuels even though they "do not use fossil fuels in the territory of the archdiocese." I suppose it is remotely possible that the archdiocese does not use electricity for its churches or its lovely cathedral and that its parish priests cook their dinners over camp stoves and read by candlelight. Maybe they run their cars on "renewable resources" like wind and sun.

The statements from the Archdiocese of Ancona-Osimo and even the Holy Father force us to ask whether these people believe basic necessities can be stored without electricity or food can be delivered by something other than gas-guzzling trucks. Certainly, in ages past meat was stored by covering it in salt or submerging it in oil. But is the Catholic Left really calling us to a more primitive age, or do they truly believe we can achieve zero fossil fuels by replacing them with windmills and solar panels?

Surely, the Catholic faithful are not required to go along with what appears to many as crunchy-chewy leftism. Catholics are utterly free to ignore the policy prescriptions of left-wing political activists, even when they dress themselves up religiously.

All of this leads us to the Paris Climate Accord, which to many on the excitable Catholic Left is nothing less than the magisterial document of an ecumenical council. Prior to the final governmental negotiations in Paris, the heads of six continental bishops' conferences, along with leaders of national conferences in the United States and Canada and Catholic patriarchs of the Orient, issued a collective statement: "We join the Holy Father in pleading for a major breakthrough in Paris, for a comprehensive and transformational agreement supported by all based on principles of solidarity, justice and participation." The statement called on governmental leaders to "strongly limit a global temperature increase." The bishops said, "Central to this is to put an end to the fossil fuel era, phasing out fossil fuel emissions in providing affordable, reliable and safe renewable energy access for all."

It is perhaps disheartening to some that the statement of these bishops and indeed parts of *Laudato si'* read as if they were negotiating documents produced at UN headquarters in Manhattan. As one would expect from a UN document, the Paris climate agreement produced remarkably unworkable and even silly goals, including "holding the increase in global average temperature to well below 2°C above preindustrial levels and to pursue efforts to limit temperature increase to 1.5°C above preindustrial levels." The document called for a 20 percent reduction in carbon dioxide emissions, a 20 percent increase in renewable energy market share, and a 20 percent increase in energy efficiency.

President Barack Obama was enthusiastically on board. He signed the document and proposed to reduce U.S. greenhouse gases by 26 percent to 28 percent below 2005 levels by the year 2025. To meet this goal, Obama promised carbon dioxide regulations for new and existing power plants, fuel efficiency and greenhouse gas regulations for light- and heavy-duty vehicles, energy efficiency regulations for commercial and residential buildings as well as appliances, EPA-approved alternatives to hydrochlorofluorocarbons, methane regulations for landfills in the oil and gas sector, and executive orders to reduce greenhouse gas emissions by the federal government. As I described in my book *Fake Science*, "President Obama proposed waging war on the carbon dioxide–emitting fuels—coal, oil, and natural gas—that have supplied the overwhelming majority of our energy needs in the past decades, in fact over the past century."

These outlandish goals come at real human cost. The Heritage Foundation estimated disaster would follow Obama's plan, and that it would result in the loss of more than 200,000 manufacturing jobs. The report predicted 400,000 fewer jobs in the United States, an income loss of $20,000 for a family of four, a GDP loss of over $2.5 trillion to the American economy, and an increase of household electricity expenditures of between 13 percent and 20 percent. To make matters worse, it's altogether unclear that any of the stated measures would have any discernible effect on global temperature. While the agreement made an awful lot of people feel good about themselves, its implementation would have caused financial ruin for millions of Americans.

Seeing the agreement as an unmitigated and unpopular disaster, candidate Trump promised to pull the United States out of the Paris

Accord. He had made numerous other campaign pledges to roll back regulations on energy production that had been imposed by Barack Obama with his "pen and his phone," but this was a big one. In June 2017, Trump made it official, announcing that he would pull the United States out of the agreement. The American Civil Liberties Union said withdrawal from the Paris agreement was "an assault on communities of color." Disagreeing with this particular solution to "man-made catastrophic climate change" was now racist. Trump was no better than Sheriff Bull Connor siccing the dogs on civil rights marchers. A Vatican official said this was "a disaster for everyone." For his part, Trump said he was "elected to represent the citizens of Pittsburgh, not Paris."

Is it a violation of Church teaching to withdraw from the Paris Climate Accord? Certainly not, but this is not all that Trump has done to anger and alarm the environmental Left, including the Catholic Left, some Bishops, and maybe even the Holy Father.

Before listing some of Trump's supposed environmental crimes, I want to touch briefly on a theme that has recurred in this book: Whenever the Left wins a victory of some sort, you can never go back. Like the Soviet Union, any ground gained can never be relinquished. For the Left, it is always more and more, higher and higher, farther and farther. And they think this is Catholic social teaching. If the minimum wage is $7.50, then Catholic social teaching says it must be $8.00. If it's $8.00, Catholic social teaching says it must be $10.00. The same with the environment. If you close off federal land to oil extraction, it is a violation of Church teaching to open it back up. This is an utterly false notion of Catholic social teaching. When Trump ratchets back some two-year-old executive order of Barack Obama's, the Catholic Left always says Church teaching is being violated. So, what has Trump done?

Many publications keep what is, practically speaking, a death-watch for the many environmental degradations of Donald Trump. In December 2019, the *New York Times*, in conjunction with Harvard Law School and the Columbia University School of Law, counted more than ninety environmental rules and regulations rolled back under President Trump. At that time, they estimated fifty-eight rollbacks had been completed while another thirty-seven were still in progress. The report said sixteen rules governing air pollution and emissions had been overturned, seven related to animals, five dealing with toxic substances, and four related to water pollution. The Catholic voter who might be skeptical of the claims of the Left may in good conscience see these changes as acceptable aspects of Catholic social teaching, which calls for the common good. The common good includes gasoline prices, for instance, that allow working men and women to drive to work. So, do not fall for the claim that Catholic social teaching requires radical environmental policies.

The thing that could very well stick in the craw of environmental scolds, both outside and inside the Church, in Roman collars and not, is the fact that U.S. greenhouse gases are down under President Trump. In fact, they are at levels almost identical to those in 1990. Certainly, the United States produces an enormous amount of Co2, more than any other country except for China. But we are the world's preeminent industrial power. This is what happens when you produce goods and services and take them to market. It is simply unrealistic for bishops and the Holy Father to suggest that we go back to subsistence farming and small fishing villages and reduce our "greenhouse" gases to zero. Quite frankly, if we did that, not only would the poor starve, but so would millions of others.

To be sure, many countries in our world are doing terrible things to the environment, and these often-necessary enormities have also caused harm to the people living there. Consider that upwards of a billion people in the world do not have access to clean water or safe sanitation. Consider that some cities in China look much like our own Los Angeles looked fifty years ago, a smog-clouded hellscape.

One can look at the history of the United States to see what runaway and uncaring industrial practice can bring. Waterways in some of our cities were unusable for decades, while the air was close to unbreathable. Calls for environmental stewardship are right and true and must be heeded. But we have done that, and we continue to do that, and Donald Trump does not propose to turn that around and make our air and water dirty again.

Catholics ought to take heart by looking at the United States and most European countries and realizing environmental stewardship can be achieved. But at the same time, that doesn't mean we have to draw the same lines as the apocalyptic Left. Leftists want to abolish the use of fossil fuels. And to whip up support for their project, they make unbelievable doomsday claims.

None of these criticisms should be read as in any way mocking or disrespecting our Holy Father, though lefty Catholics charge critics as anti-Francis heretics if they part his company on global catastrophic climate change. But even the Holy Father in *Laudato si'* makes one thing abundantly clear, and global warming skeptics in the Church must hold fast to this: he says correctly that the Church cannot settle scientific questions. Let that sink in. The Church cannot settle scientific claims, even those the pope himself believes in.

So, to disagree with these empirical and scientific assertions is not to disagree with any teachings of the Church. Faithful Catholics will completely agree we have a responsibility to care for the environment, but we are not required to believe in man-made catastrophic climate change, or even that the harmful warming of the planet is caused by fossil fuels. It is conceivable that our levels of CO_2 could affect climate, but how much, nobody knows.

As in many matters, the Church allows for prudential judgments on how to proceed. That the Holy Father criticizes air-conditioning does not mean we have to shut it off. That the Holy Father believes in global catastrophic climate change does not mean we have to agree. The Catholic Left wants us to believe that *Laudato si'* is Church dogma, when the document itself explicitly denies that. The Church allows for vociferous debates on matters of public policy. We have to care for God's creation, which reflects his glory. Amen. All Catholics can agree with that teaching of the Church. How do we go about it? That is up to us. Donald Trump has his way, and his way is not in opposition to essential Church teaching.

CHAPTER EIGHT

Trump and Racism

In February 2016, during the hottest time of the GOP primaries, candidate Trump retweeted something from an account going by the Twitter handle @ilduce2016. Look closely and you may notice the words "Il Duce," the name Italian dictator Benito Mussolini fashioned for himself. "Better to live one day as a lion, than 100 years as a sheep," Trump retweeted. Gotcha! Trump was quoting Mussolini from a Mussolini account.

As it turns out, the account was created precisely to lure retweets from Trump that the media could smear him with. The brainchild of two staffers from the now disgraced and shuttered website Gawker, a site hated equally by Left and Right for the smarminess of its coverage, the idea shows a lot about how racism charges against Donald Trump work. The Gawker article said, "We set a trap for Trump. We came up with the idea for that Mussolini bot under the assumption that Trump would retweet just about anything, no matter how dubious or violent the source, as long as it sounded like praise for himself."

Like clockwork, the legacy media jumped on the issue. A few days later, on NBC's *Meet the Press*, former Democratic staffer and now-host Chuck Todd pushed Trump, "That's a famous Mussolini quote, you retweeted it. Do you like the quote? Did you know it was Mussolini?"

An exquisitely orchestrated gotcha moment. Did Trump know that the Italian dictator used that quote? Was Trump a fascist? This fit perfectly into two left-wing narratives about Trump. On the one hand, the Left revels in Trump's supposed lack of book learning; on the other, Trump is a fascist who wants to be a dictator. There was also a third narrative, one aimed at voters: if you support Trump, you support fascism.

It should be understood that although Mussolini perhaps used the quote, it was not his. Yes, it was attributed to him, but it was also attributed to an unknown Italian soldier and the graffiti he scrawled on a wall. It has also been attributed to Alexander the Great and, according to the *Oxford Dictionary of Proverbs*, to the sultan of a place called Mysore circa 1799. No matter, it was a classic political dirty trick carried out with the eager cooperation of the left-wing media. But in comparison to the efforts that the Left continues to use to present Trump as a brownshirt white nationalist, this would come to look rather mild.

Calling Trump a racist is now a veritable cottage industry. The Wikipedia article on the "Racial views of Donald Trump" runs to a whopping 41 pages and includes 315 footnotes as of February 2020. It will no doubt have grown by the time you read this.

The charge of racism is a form of what I call "political Tourette's," a practically involuntary verbal tic used to smear anyone who may disagree with the Left. While conservatives know that that trick has been going on for decades, Democrats have deployed it with new zeal against President Trump. Even worse, they don't stop at Trump; they suggest that his supporters are racist too.

The Left calls Donald Trump racist because he refuses to conform to their standards of political correctness. That was true before he was president and only accelerated after Trump declared his candidacy for our nation's highest office. The Left changed what it means to be "racist" and has inculcated a new standard of racism in our popular culture. If you reject their moral claims, and in some cases even their policy prescriptions that have nothing to do with race, they'll try to cudgel you into submission by stoking racial tensions. That's not only un-American, it's un-Christian.

Let's start by discussing some of the accusations leftists made against Trump before his time in politics. A major part of the case against Trump is the full-page ad he took out in 1989 calling for the death penalty for five young blacks who rampaged through Central Park one night and, among other things, were charged with the violent rape and near murder of a female jogger. A serial rapist later admitted to the rape and the Central Park Five were "exonerated." In 2014, the city, under hard-left mayor Bill de Blasio, paid them $41 million. Trump called the settlement a "disgrace," and it was, because those five young men did in fact rampage through the park and assault numerous innocent bystanders. They admitted it. What's more, according to a panel convened by then–police commissioner Raymond Kelly, the young men might not have raped the woman, but they were involved in an assault against her and, we emphasize, many others that night.

The progressive Left canonized the Central Park Five, and Donald Trump's refusal to pray to them made him a heretic. That's why they called him a racist: the Central Park Five were beyond reproach and Trump had the audacity to refuse to repent for siding with law and order. Most of the charges against Trump, though, are because he similarly refused to be shaken down by racial interest groups during his time in the private sector. In the 1970s, New York City and the Justice Department went after twenty-seven-year-old Trump for discriminating against blacks in renting apartments. In the end, Trump's company was ordered to report vacancies each week to the Urban League. Trump denied the charges, and as is his wont, countersued the government for hundreds of millions of dollars. Blacks went after Trump in Gary, Indiana, for not hiring 70 percent of his floating casino employees from the black community. Moreover, local black contractors tried to shake down Trump for their "fair share" of the construction work.

Building trades are rife with such controversies, agreements in hiring, sweetheart deals, labor strife, and lawsuits. Trump came up in one of the most raucous and cutthroat real estate environments in the world. It is not a clean business and is utterly foreign to the experience of most Americans. Trump has the scars and the judgments, for and against, to prove it. Using discrimination law is a powerful tool at the negotiating table, where everyone is looking for leverage to use against the other side. Calling Trump a racist allowed the people Trump was doing business with to negotiate for more or get a better deal in the future.

In the 1990s, Trump was in a pitched battle with an Indian tribe and its casino. Indian casinos are exempt from paying federal and state taxes, a fact which rankled Trump the businessman. He felt it was an unfair practice. While Trump was paying hundreds of millions in taxes, his competitors didn't owe Uncle Sam a single cent. He got in trouble when he told a Senate committee that the owners of the St. Regis Mohawk tribe's casino "did not look like Indians" while complaining that the FBI was crawling all over Las Vegas but did not have a single field agent assigned to investigating the Native American casinos. That's not racism, that's fighting a competitor who has a seriously unfair advantage. Recall also that Elizabeth Warren got a free pass for pretending to be an Indian and arguing that her "Paw-Paw" and his high cheekbones looked Indian.

We live in a highly charged racial society where charges of racism are leveled promiscuously. Is it racist not to hire 70 percent blacks for a casino? Is it racist to say a group of Indians don't appear to be Indians? No. But when race becomes a weapon to advance yourself economically, judicially, and politically while denigrating your political opponents, "racism" loses any meaningful sense.

Unsurprisingly, the Left didn't target Trump for these alleged wrongdoings until he became a Republican. Once Trump entered the political arena as a figure on the Right, they tried to dredge up whatever racism accusations they could find to sully his name. All the while, leftists started working double time to create the narrative that Donald Trump was an ethno-fascist who wanted to bring back the Ku Klux Klan. From the moment Donald Trump took that escalator ride in Trump Tower to announce his candidacy, he has been called a racist for nearly everything he does.

Fighting illegal immigration was one of Trump's signature issues. That doesn't make him racist, it means that he stands for the rule of law. Millions of Americans have been harmed by the chaos on our southern border, whether from the influx of violent criminals, illegal drugs, or cheap labor. The Left, as well as the bipartisan elite in Washington, profited from that situation, so when Donald Trump called them to account, they shirked responsibility by denouncing him as racist.

After the election, it was reported that Trump described some countries as "shitholes." Though Trump denied the reports, the actual phrasing he used is irrelevant. According to his accusers, it was racist because it referred to Haiti, which, truth be told, is an utter and complete disaster.

Trump likewise called Baltimore "disgusting" and "rodent infested" while in a war of words with the late hyper-racialist Congressman Elijah Cummings. But is recognizing that Baltimore, long one of the most dangerous cities in America, is in terrible shape really racism? While Trump's comment turned out to be true, his crime was really violating political correctness. Elijah Cummings had represented that district for years while it steadily deteriorated under his watch. Perhaps abiding by the politically correct standards liberals enforce is part of the reason why things seem to go from bad to worse in that struggling city.

Among the most incendiary and false narratives about Trump is that he described neo-Nazis and white supremacists as "very fine people." This charge gets into the question of narratives that refuse to go away no matter how many times they are shown to be false. To Democrats in the business of smearing their opponents, giving an honest accounting of events matters less than framing facts in a politically advantageous context, no matter how divorced that context is from reality. While the Left has consistently done this against Donald Trump from his first days as a presidential candidate, leftists have also done the same thing to conservatives for decades. Looking at the Charlottesville incident is thus instructive in how Democrats and the media use deliberate falsehoods to demonize their political opposition.

For those who may not recall, the controversy in Charlottesville surrounded protests against the removal of a statue of General Robert E. Lee. At that time, the Left was on an iconoclastic spree of tearing down statues of figures from our country's past, some with better cause than others. The issue revved up in Charlottesville when the city council voted to remove a giant statue of Lee in a downtown park. While thousands of people showed up to peacefully express their views on the matter, some violent extremists from both the Right and the Left decided to use the occasion as a platform to gain national attention. Oddball white supremacist organizations made their presence known, as did Antifa activists looking for a fight. Chaos predictably broke out, and a young woman lost her life when a man linked to a white nationalist group hit her with his car.

President Trump was called upon to respond almost immediately in a frenzied scene in the lobby of Trump Tower. In his remarks, Trump told reporters that he saw the riot as two-sided, with the neo-Nazis on one side who lined up against Antifa on the other, both of whom came at each other with clubs and other weapons. But Trump also saw another group in the mix—the people who came to peacefully protest removing the statue, the ones who didn't want to fight but wanted their voices to be heard.

And then he said this: "[A]nd you had very bad people in that group, you also had people that were very fine people, on both sides.... You had people in that group that were there to protest the taking down of, to them, a very, very important statue and the renaming of a park from Robert E. Lee to another name. And you had people," Trump continued, "and I'm not talking about the neo-Nazis and the white nationalists, because they should be condemned totally. But you had many people in that group other than neo-Nazis and white nationalists. Okay? And the press has treated them absolutely unfairly." Trump went on to say, "Racism is evil, and those who caused violence in its name are criminals and thugs, including the KKK, neo-Nazis, white supremacists, and other hate groups that are repugnant to everything we hold dear as Americans."

Trump repeatedly made it clear that he was talking about the peaceful protesters when he spoke of "very fine people," but the mainstream media and the American Left didn't want to hear that. To this day, journalists and Democrats routinely say that Trump called neo-Nazis "very fine people." In fact, when Joe Biden announced his run for the presidency he began with this slander against Trump. No matter how many times Trump condemns racism and racists, the narrative will not die.

Donald Trump's supporters absolutely love that he refuses to back down and hits back hard. Sometimes that can get him in trouble, but it's served him quite well throughout his time in the political arena. By the time Donald Trump came around, Republicans had grown tired of "Gentleman Jim" candidates who refused to fight back, even against outrageous slanders perpetrated by their political opponents and the media. Just look at Mitt Romney's nonresponse when the Obama campaign said that his policies would "drive granny over the cliff." He refused to fight back. George Bush was the same way, and so was his father. Republicans were becoming punching bags in mainstream culture, a pose that began to look more cowardly than gentlemanly.

The Republican establishment didn't understand that as messy as Trump could get, GOP voters were weary of cowardly Republicans who refused to take on the Left's stifling political correctness.

Perhaps he could have handled some issues a little more delicately, but Trump's supporters, even his Catholic supporters, were willing to look beyond it because, as President Lincoln said about General Ulysses S. Grant, "Here is a man who fights."

Our hyper-racialized time has made it so that you need a college degree in order to define what racism is. Today, it is considered racist to oppose race-based quotas in hiring and college admissions. It's considered racist to oppose "disparate impact" standards, which force Americans to think of their fellow citizens in terms of their race only. We live in a time when blacks and other minorities can claim special spaces at universities that are off-limits to whites, and this is not considered racism. In other words, everything we usually think of as "racist," or discriminating based on race, is now fair game, while the commonsense demand that all people be treated equally is thought of as unforgivable.

You can be sure that the charge of racism will continue in the final weeks of the 2020 campaign. The charge will be further stoked by the riots now engulfing American cities even as I write these words. The Catholic voter should understand that these charges against Trump are false; I have found no genuine proof that Donald Trump is prejudiced against African Americans. The Left is doing to him what they do to you, using racism as a slanderous epithet against someone they disagree with politically. It is one of the things that has poisoned our politics over these past several decades. I would even go so far as to venture this guess: Donald Trump will win more black votes in November than he did last time, and more than any GOP candidate in recent memory. I am convinced that everyday men and women of all races see in Donald Trump a man who truly cares.

CHAPTER NINE

Trump the Statesman

There is a general misunderstanding that "statesman" means only one thing: a man who acts and speaks for etchings on marble, who acts and speaks for the ages. In fact, a statesman is a man who advances the cause of his country on the world stage. He may speak in dulcet tones. He may speak in purple vulgarity. But above all, a statesman works to advance the national interest as he sees fit. Sometimes, his words and actions go against the consensus of foreign policy elites. This makes him no less statesmanlike. In fact, it's often a good thing. Trump is such a statesman, perhaps rough around the edges, perhaps maddening to friends and allies, but only his sworn domestic enemies—the NeverTrumpers on the Left and Right—believe he has anything other than his country at heart.

Trump has staked out positions that his predecessors have been either unwilling or too fearful to take. Perhaps they have simply lacked the imagination to advance them. Whether talking about

Mexico, China, Iran, Syria, or Russia, Trump believes he alone can make magic out of a mess. Just get me in a room with the guy and I can make it all better, he thinks. While Trump is not the only president who has believed this (most of them do), Trump knows that he is uniquely capable of making deals. Deals are what he has lived for.

When the "experts" tell him he can't do something, he is only more motivated to prove them wrong. Which real estate "expert" would have thought that a brash twenty-seven-year-old with a Queens apartment building pedigree and accent to boot would be able to develop the Commodore Hotel near Grand Central Station? Which one of them would have thought that Trump would become a heavyweight in the Manhattan luxury real estate scene? Yet despite the doubters, Trump pulled those deals off with the same qualities that lead him to believe in himself on the world stage. In the same way, he looks at various international situations and sees new ways to approach them, often in contradistinction from the foreign policy consensus. And he always thinks he can make a deal where others failed.

Before Trump took office, Barack Obama warned him that North Korea was an intractable and perhaps unsolvable problem. Indeed, North Korea has been the epicenter of failure for American bipartisan foreign policy for decades.

Trump initiated what many saw as a very unstatesmanlike, undiplomatic war of words with the North Korean dictator. Trump threatened the North Koreans with "fire and fury unlike anything the world has ever seen." Responding to Kim Jong-un's claim that the nuclear button was on his desk at all times, Trump tweeted, "Will someone from his depleted and food starved regime please inform him that I too have a Nuclear Button, but it is a much bigger & more powerful one than his, and my Button works!" Trump also took to calling the North Korean leader "Little Rocket Man." Foreign policy paladins and their pals in the media were appalled. How statesmanlike is that?

They were even more appalled when only a few months later, Trump announced he would become the first sitting U.S. president to meet face-to-face with a North Korean leader. It stunned the world and certainly members of the bipartisan U.S. foreign policy consensus. What a dangerous fool, they thought. All prior talks at every level were generally preceded by months and even years of diplomatic preparation. Trump gave his team only a few months to prepare. The North Korean foreign minister had said that under no circumstances would North Korea's nuclear program, now much further advanced because of the failure of previous U.S. presidents, be put on the negotiating table.

Trump's meeting was a ringing success, though it may not have solved the North Korean debacle once and for all. No less a left-wing rag than *The Atlantic* admitted that Trump "racked up real accomplishments" and that "the United States and the world are safer now than they were before he decided to become the first American president to meet with North Korea's leader."

North Korean expert Nicholas Eberstadt of the American Enterprise Institute says Trump's "maximum pressure" campaign of 2017–2018 "is the closest thing to a strategy for crippling North Korea's war economy that Washington has devised to date."

When Kim Jong-un tried to extract big concessions from Trump in the lead-up to a second meeting, Trump called things off. Trump got the sense that Kim Jong-un thought he was desperate to make a deal, while, if anything, the reverse was true. So, instead of caving to whatever outlandish demands Little Rocket Man made, Trump backed away, showing that American foreign policy was back in the hands of a pragmatist who was only interested in making deals that benefit the American people. Could it be that the "unstatesmanlike" Trump has made more progress with North Korea in a few months than his predecessors had in decades?

President Trump has likewise demonstrated his ability to act on the world stage in his interactions with Russia. According to his ridiculous NeverTrump opponents, Trump is a Russian asset. He supposedly colluded with Vladimir Putin in stealing the election away from Hillary Clinton, a charge now thoroughly debunked by the Mueller Report. But who was soft on Russia? Who let Russia get away with murder? Russia didn't declare war on its neighboring state of Georgia during the Trump presidency; that was under George W. Bush's watch. And it was during the golden years of the Obama administration that Russia took over Crimea and attacked the Donbass region of Ukraine. Obama responded by putting some

Russian oligarchs on a sanctions list and sending Ukrainians socks and blankets. Recall also that Barack Obama was heard on a hot mic telling then–Russian president Dimitri Medvedev that after his election he would have more flexibility in caving in to Russian demands on missile defense in Europe. He asked Medvedev to pass the information "along to Vlad."

Trump took the opposite approach. Instead of talking a big game at home about Russia while quietly enabling Russian troublemaking, Trump spoke softly toward Putin and sent lethal weapons to Putin's enemies, the Ukrainians.

There is genius behind Trump's approach to Russia. Foreign policy expert J. Michael Waller of the Center for Security Policy says Trump's soft rhetoric toward Russia masks an assertiveness towards Putin, and that Trump has denied what the Kremlin wants most, an external enemy. Trump initiated a new National Security Strategy that incorporated many hard-line initiatives. He increased military spending and restored the old policy of "peace through strength." He shamed NATO allies into ratcheting up their defense spending. He also pushed European countries to stop Putin's Nord Stream 2 gas pipeline that would have made Germany oil-dependent on Putin. This, coupled with unleashing domestic oil and gas exploration, has directly threatened the economy of Russia and made the United States the number one fossil fuel exporter in the world. Where Obama abolished the Navy's Second Fleet, Trump restored it in order to intercept Russian subs off of our Atlantic coast. Trump views Russia as a sometimes-strategic partner, but there is little doubt that he has taken a much more aggressive role in blocking Russian influence around the world.

Perhaps the most interesting recent development that has flummoxed the foreign policy establishment is Trump's policy toward our old enemy, Iran.

Trump's unilateral determination to pull out of the Iranian nuclear arms deal caused grave concern to lots of foreign policy experts. Trump, like most Americans, viewed the deal as a direct threat to our ally Israel and a way for American taxpayers to fund Iranian hegemony in the region. When Iran started to act up, President Trump didn't hesitate to put them back in their place by authorizing a strike on Iranian general Qasem Soleimani. The foreign policy establishment, the largely left-wing media, and the Democratic candidates for president panicked. They said World War III was upon us and that it had been initiated by the unhinged madman Donald Trump. But that war, as we all know, never happened.

Once again, even left-wing outlets such as *The Atlantic* were forced to admit that Trump had scored a major foreign policy victory: "[W]hether by accident or design, Trump creates chances to solve long-running international problems that a conventional leader would not." No less an authority than Henry Kissinger echoed that sentiment, saying, "I think Trump may be one of those figures in history who appears from time to time to mark the end of an era and to force it to give up its old pretense."

The killing of the Iranian commander reminded the world that the United States is still in the driver's seat. While Trump is understandably eager to bring more American troops home, that does not mean he'll tolerate threats to American personnel stationed around the world. If you threaten the lives of American citizens, you better be prepared to take some serious pain yourself.

Trump has worked hard to bring credibility back to America's threats. Previous administrations were too worried about stepping on toes to get things done in the international sphere. President Trump, meanwhile, knows that being willing to play rough commands the respect of our adversaries and allies alike. That, more than sweet words, guarantees Americans' safety and helps prevent the use of lethal force.

Nowhere have these principles been clearer than in the Trump administration's negotiations with China. Successive American leaders kowtowed to the Communist dictators in Beijing, allowing them to manipulate their currency, steal American intellectual property, and undercut the American labor force. They negotiated trade deals deeply harmful to the American worker. Trump joked that he was the "chosen one" to deal with the Chinese trade issue, and his trade war with China has certainly scrambled the deck. The coronavirus disaster only underscores the dangers of maintaining an extensive supply chain of goods from China, validating Trump's concerns that were the butt of establishment jokes just a few years ago.

I remember in the '80s when American businessmen learned how to bow slightly and subserviently offer their business cards with two hands to their dominant Japanese counterparts. American business has acted the same way toward China in recent years. Liberal Hollywood, always willing to pronounce the most hare-brained condemnations of the United States, refused to make movies critical of China out of hunger for the massive Chinese market. While Hollywood may not have changed its tune, Donald Trump is bringing an end to American business selling us out in its pursuit of Chinese markets. When he secured his Phase One trade deal, President Trump showed concrete proof that he could bring home the bacon by getting deals across the line that experts had long considered impossible. When Trump ran for office, opening trade negotiations with China was thought of as an undeliverable campaign promise. As Trump heads into his re-election bid, he has signed a deal with China that commits them to buying billions of dollars of American goods. Quite a statesmanlike accomplishment, if you ask me.

Without a doubt, Trump is an unusual statesman. He has upset the long-standing foreign policy consensus. He has ended U.S. participation in various multilateral venues, most especially the United Nations. He has withdrawn the United States from the United Nations Human Rights Council. He has reduced American funding to various human rights bodies. He has bad-mouthed NATO and our European allies. He has questioned the necessity of American troops being stationed in more than 700 locations around the world. He is annoyed that this defense umbrella is paid for exclusively by the American taxpayer. When he brings up remuneration to the United States for this defense umbrella, he is criticized for trying to turn our soldiers into mercenaries. And while some foreign leaders are deeply embarrassed by President Trump, especially diplomatic types in Great Britain, France, and Germany, one need only see 125,000 Indians jam into a Delhi cricket stadium to see the disjunction between elites and the people.

Catholics have wildly divergent views on foreign policy. There is no Catholic teaching on the specifics of our country's relationship with Russia, China, Iran, North Korea, or any other country. The Church does not have a teaching on specific theories of foreign policy except in so far as we believe in subsidiarity, that policies should be determined by the smallest possible denomination of society, beginning with the family.

While particular relations with foreign governments may be outside the scope of the Catholic Church's teaching, the Church does have dozens of political teachings on the conduct of foreign affairs. Through the lens of those teachings, we can assess Trump's "America First" philosophy and his views on war and defense, which seek increased prosperity and well-being for American citizens. Looked at in this light, we can say with confidence that President Trump has conducted himself in foreign affairs in accord with standards Catholics ought to accept.

After a long period of subordination of U.S. national priorities to globalization initiatives, Trump promised to reverse policies that sub-optimized conditions for success. Trump rejected the trend toward increased military hegemony, unnecessary war, war waged without clearly stated strategic objectives, and inequitable defense burden arrangements with allies. In Trump's view, wars that are not critical to vital U.S. national interests are costly and harmful, not worth their cost in American blood and treasure. He has a high threshold for war, something even the Catholic Left should embrace.

War has often been a thorny issue for Catholics who are politically conservative. Pope John Paul II, for instance, vocally opposed George Bush's adventurism in Iraq. In the strongest possible terms, he said that the Iraq War was a mistake and would have massive unintended consequences for the region and for religious believers in Iraq. While I was a supporter of George Bush and the Iraq War, I, alongside many initial supporters of the war, now see that the pope was right. It should be pointed out, however, that the pope never said the war was unjust according to Catholic teaching. Certainly, he sent his emissaries to the White House to speak strongly against the war. It is said that one of his emissaries, Cardinal Pio Laghi, the papal nuncio to the United States, used the word "unjust," but this word was never uttered by the pope himself. Politically liberal Catholics often exploit the general opposition of the Vatican toward war as a way to criticize Republicans. This is often done as a way to cover over the Democrats' support for killing the unborn.

And then there was the issue of waterboarding Islamic terrorists. This was the practice of pouring water over the covered face of a person being interrogated, causing the sensation of drowning. It was argued in certain Catholic circles that the Republicans favored torture, which is forbidden in international law and also in Catholic teaching. There was an ongoing debate about whether waterboarding constituted torture, which I will not revisit here. As it happened, only three terrorist suspects were waterboarded. The Catholic Left wants voters to believe that waterboarding three terrorists somehow stacks up against hundreds of thousands of abortions a year. This is their argument anyway, though I consider it nothing more than a political dodge.

When it comes to war, though, do the Democrats really have less blood on their hands than the Republicans? Donald Trump, it's important to note, ran against a bipartisan consensus of American foreign policy, advanced just as much by Barack Obama and Bill Clinton as by the Bush family. Perhaps the best place to start, then, is comparing the actions of Barack Obama and his secretary of state Hillary Clinton to those of Trump in the first years of his presidency.

While Barack Obama may have played the peacenik for the cameras, he was deeply committed to war in practice. It should also be pointed out that Obama bombed more countries using drones than any other president in history, with hardly a peep from the political Left. Moreover, in the Oval Office Obama frequently referred to a kill list—called the "disposition matrix"—from which he would personally choose targets. This list included at least one American citizen he chose for what the Catholic Left would call assassination. This American citizen was certainly a traitor to his country and helping to lead a terrorist organization. But he was an

American citizen nonetheless, and the decision to kill him extrajudicially by drone strike certainly flies in the face of everything the Catholic Left preaches. This is not to say that what Obama did was wrong, only that it fails to meet the moral standard to which the Catholic Left holds Republicans. It should also be pointed out that Barack Obama and Hillary Clinton bombed the country of Libya nonstop for eight months, destroying the country and turning it into a haven for terrorist organizations.

It is abundantly clear that these left-wing commentators are eager to demoralize Catholic voters by portraying Republicans as unabashed warmongers. The charge, often implicit, is that Trump has violated Catholic just war teaching and it is therefore against the faith to vote for him. So, the argument goes, voting for Democrats who subsidize the killing of the unborn by the thousands is permissible. This calculation simply does not work for the faithful Catholic.

Without a doubt, Catholics must take just war theory to heart. Just war theory's origin, in the Catholic tradition, was in North Africa with St. Augustine. There are hundreds of volumes dedicated to this theory, but, in short, it states that the prosecution of a just war requires a just cause. It must be waged by legitimate authority. It must be in self-defense or the defense of others. The response should be proportionate. And there should be a reasonable expectation of victory.

It should be pointed out that Catholic just war theory does not require the consent of the U.S. Congress for carrying out surgical strikes against aggressors. Nor does it require getting permission from the UN Security Council or NBC News. It's not a procedural exposition, but a theoretical account of the cases in which war is morally defensible.

As evidenced above, some Catholic theologians and other lefty activist types cannot be counted on to be serious about just war theory and how the United States should protect itself, our allies, and innocents. As George Weigel put it during the Iraq War, which tactically speaking he was wrong about, the best repository for serious thinking about Catholic just war theory is not the Catholic academy, the U.S. Conference of Catholic Bishops, or even the various dicasteries of the Holy See. It is in the service academies of the U.S. military. Our officer corps is the only group that still takes these issues seriously.

So, where has Donald Trump found success in the application of military force? For starters, he has fulfilled his promise to wipe out the caliphate of the Islamic State of Iraq and Syria (ISIS). And he did this with all due dispatch—at practically lightning speed.

ISIS was a cancerous terror growth of Al-Qaeda that was allowed to fester, grow, and even prosper after President Obama bugged out of Iraq in 2011. Three years later, on January 27, 2014, Obama blithely dismissed ISIS as the "JV team." At its height, the ISIS caliphate, Obama's junior varsity, measured the size of Britain and controlled the lives of upwards of 12 million people, a remarkable conquest in only a few years. Most of this occurred thanks to Obama's flawed policy-making decisions. Obama gave radical

Islamists the space and time to regenerate. And the result was both astounding and profoundly dangerous to the region and to the United States.

At its height, the Islamic State spanned from Mosul, the second-largest city in Iraq, to Palmyra, the ruins of an ancient city in Syria. It didn't take long for the Obama administration to get serious about the "junior varsity" team, eventually working with regional allies to take back territory ISIS had conquered and issuing air strikes in support of that mission. But Obama did not have a strategy for defeating ISIS. In fact, his efforts only seemed to exacerbate the situation. One of the essential problems was that Obama and his men micromanaged efforts against ISIS from the Situation Room of the White House. Remember, Obama had a kill list in his desk from which he would determine who would get bombed. This level of micromanagement hampered our efforts in Syria, Iraq, and Afghanistan, and it puts one in mind of the micromanaging that went on in Lyndon Johnson's White House during the Vietnam War, where civilians would choose bombing targets from the safety and near blindness of 1600 Pennsylvania Avenue. I have never served in the military, and I recognize the essential nature of civilian control of the military, but I am astounded by the hubris of Obama pajama boys, like the former novelist Ben Rhodes, who think they can sit in judgment of the commanders on the ground.

By the time Trump took office, wars were raging in both Iraq and Syria thanks to the Obama administration's incompetence. And then came Trump. Days after his inauguration, Trump issued an executive order directing the Pentagon to come up with a plan on how ISIS could be defeated.

As the Heritage Foundation reported, "tactical tweaks did quickly begin to appear." Secretary of Defense James Mattis said Trump intended to delegate "authority to the right level to aggressively and in a timely manner move against enemy vulnerabilities." In ordinary language, commanders on the ground were given the flexibility to make decisions on their own. They did not have to get a number of sign-offs to bomb ISIS targets. Imagine some left-wing pencil-neck in the White House with his slide rule deciding where the tough guys ought to target American power, while you and your cohort wait in the trenches. That's not fighting with the intent to win.

Ten months after Trump's inauguration, the chairman of the Joint Chiefs of Staff announced, "We don't see large numbers of fighters coming out of Syria and Iraq. The numbers that we're seeing in other places that have come from Syria and Iraq are fairly small." That is because they were getting killed by American forces and our allies, who had been unleashed by Donald Trump. President Trump made sure that the American military was able to do more with less. By making sure the business of waging war was left to those who are trained in it, without interference from staffers halfway across the globe, Trump led us to victory.

Trump's change in the rules of engagement did not come without criticism. With increased bombing came increased civilian casualties and the not-unexpected charges of mistakes and indiscriminate targeting. Still, it must be pointed out that U.S. bombing under Trump has remained highly targeted. Though decision-making has passed to commanders on the ground, there is no evidence that bombing has been indiscriminate. U.S. bombing and even the unintentional killing of noncombatants remains within the bounds of established international laws of war.

Under Trump, the geographical caliphate has been utterly destroyed. By the end of his first year in office, the Trump administration had liberated twice as many people and 18 percent more territory than in the previous twenty-eight months of the Obama administration. On the day Trump was inaugurated, it was estimated that 35,000 ISIS fighters held roughly 17,500 square miles of territory in Iraq and Syria. By the end of the year Trump had liberated 15,570 square miles and 5.3 million people.

It is quite remarkable what can happen when a leader begins to defer to his military experts rather than second-guessing their decisions on the ground. After the fall of Mosul came a series of victories in other towns, culminating in what has been described as a crushing blow to the Islamic State's other capital, Raqqa. One battlefield commander said, "We don't get second-guessed a lot. Our judgment here on the battlefield in the forward areas is trusted. And we don't get 20 questions with every action that happens on the battlefield and every action that we take. Commanders are not constantly calling back to higher headquarters asking for permission. They're free to act."

After the final little town held by ISIS fell, Trump said, "To all the young people on the Internet believing in ISIS's propaganda, you will be dead. Think instead about having a great life. While on occasion these cowards will resurface, they have lost all prestige and power. They are losers and will always be losers." Some will say this is his usual childish blather and that such pronouncements will only have the effect of rejuvenating the enemy. To many of us, it is both comical and a much-appreciated dose of the truth. To hell with the Islamists. Rub their noses in it.

There is nothing inherently un-Catholic about Donald Trump's wartime rhetoric. The Left and even some conservative Catholic intellectuals have been up in arms about his extravagant claims that he would bomb the families of terrorists, for instance, or would revive enhanced interrogation techniques such as the waterboarding that happened a few times under the Bush administration. But there is nothing inherently un-Catholic about Trump's bragging and mocking enemy losses. We are led to believe we live in an age of calm, measured, and even academic language. As far as I know, there is no admonition in Catholic teaching that we all have to speak with the measured cadence of Princeton professors.

Trump may not seem like a statesman to those who are used to the way of thoughtful Princeton professors. But even the Left is giving Trump guarded praise for his approach to foreign policy. Many of these issues are intractable, Obama was right about that. In fact, much of foreign policy is managing the intractable. And on that score, Trump, for all his warts, is doing as well or better than anyone expected, while also bringing home better results than many of his predecessors.

CHAPTER TEN

Trump and the Catholic Voter

The Catholic voter is a prized possession. And the push and pull on him is sometimes intense. We as Catholics are often subject to more pressures than other faith groups, forced to reconcile conflicting messages from the clerisy with different political impulses we may have. Choosing whom to support is a difficult enough task for anyone. It's even harder when trying to reconcile those decisions with one's faith.

Traditionally, the Catholic vote was a safe harbor for Democrats. Many working-class Catholics, often from immigrant backgrounds in our nation's great cities, held the false view that the Democrat Franklin Roosevelt saved the working man from the Great Depression. Catholics were a reliable vote for the New Deal Democrats and an important part of their coalition. But this allegiance began to waver with the Great Disruptions of the 1960s.

Catholic unrest first came to light when the new Conservative Party in New York State nominated conservative writer William F. Buckley Jr. for mayor of New York City, running against the Democrat Abe Beame and the liberal Republican John V. Lindsay. Though Buckley ran to stop Lindsay, he likely handed the election over to him by siphoning off 340,000 reliably Democrat votes from largely white, ethnic Catholic neighborhoods in the outer boroughs. While Buckley was an upper-crust Manhattanite, he had tremendous success among typically blue-collar Catholics. Catholic Democrats were starting to desert their party because of its leftward drift, and Buckley, unlike Lindsay, was able to win over their vote by focusing on the cultural issues that mattered to them.

Buckley's surprise success in the mayoral election had great impact, despite the fact that he did not win. Richard Nixon noticed that Buckley was able to win over New Deal Democrat Catholics by focusing on social issues and set out to implement Buckley's mayoral campaign strategy nationally. As if Nixon's 1968 success weren't a clear enough sign that the New Deal coalition had fractured, the 1972 election demonstrated conclusively that the Democratic coalition first forged by Franklin Roosevelt had disintegrated. Nixon carried forty-nine states and garnered 60 percent of the national vote. Nixon became the first Republican to receive a majority of the Catholic vote. As George Marlin writes in his magisterial history of the Catholic vote, *The American Catholic Voter*, "Poles in Detroit, Pittsburgh, Buffalo, and Lackawanna; Italians in Philadelphia, Boston, and Chicago; Irish in New York and

Boston; Germans in St. Paul and Milwaukee overwhelmingly endorsed Nixon."

Catholics brought Nixon his stunning victory and have voted with the winner ever since, with the exceptions of Reagan in 1980, Clinton in 1992, and Bush in 2000. As a result, Catholics have become the subject of increasingly sophisticated voter outreach campaigns conducted by Republicans and Democrats alike. In 2004, the battle for the Catholic vote heated up considerably because the Democrats did the unthinkable and nominated a dissenting Catholic— that is, an abortion proponent—to head their ticket. George Bush created an aggressive Catholic outreach that saw voter guides, often from outside groups like Priests for Life, appear on car windshields in parish parking lots in swing states. Crack teams of Catholic get-out-the-vote volunteers swarmed through Pennsylvania and Ohio.

Bush won the Catholic vote by a landslide in 2004, among both faithful Mass-going Catholics and generics—those who call themselves Catholic but only rarely practice the faith. Barack Obama answered with a Catholic effort of his own. George Soros funded two leftist Catholic outreach groups, Catholics in Alliance for the Common Good and Catholics United, both of which were squishy on the non-negotiables of abortion and marriage. Waterboarding became a salient issue for the Left. George Bush had waterboarded three terrorists, and the Catholic Left convinced at least some Catholic voters that this was proportionate to hundreds of thousands of abortions per year. Obama won the Catholic vote by 55 percent in '08 and 52 percent in '12.

The problem for Donald Trump in 2016 and for Republicans going forward is the Nixon–Reagan Democrats, the last embers of the "Greatest Generation" who were, in fact, dying rapidly by then, some say one thousand per day. Trump did not have a Catholic campaign per se. In fact, his Catholic outreach was rather pathetic. He focused most of his attention on Evangelicals. Catholics were only an afterthought or addendum to the Evangelical vote. They were included in the massive "pastors'" meeting in New York during that campaign season, but it was still largely and almost exclusively for Evangelical pastors.

Instead, as George Marlin argues, Trump focused his attention on a few closely contested Rust Belt states, and the "one or two percent difference that practicing Catholics can make would determine" the presidency. And that is what happened that November 8.

Trump had to win at least two Rust Belt states, though Ohio had voted Democrat in every election since 2004, Pennsylvania had been a firewall for Democrats since 1988, Michigan since 1988, and Wisconsin since 1984.

In 2000, Bush won Ohio with 50 percent of the vote and 50 percent of the Catholic vote. He won again in 2004 against dissenting Catholic John Kerry with 50.8 percent of the general vote but 55 percent of the Catholic vote. My personal belief is that Catholics, even nonpracticing Catholics, were uneasy with the proposition of voting for a dissenting pro-abortion Catholic for the very first time.

In 2004, when pro-abortion Catholic John Kerry was running for president, Bishop Raymond Burke, then of St. Louis, publicly announced Kerry could not receive Communion in his archdiocese. This was one of the most remarkable moments in the history of the Church in America and in politics. The Eucharist became a central part of our national political debate. That remains a first of a quite remarkable kind.

Some wring their hands at what they see as the politicization of the Eucharist. How dare someone like Burke make the Eucharist a Democratic or Republican issue? Of course, he did no such thing. What he did was announce, in accordance with St. Paul, that one may not receive Communion in an unworthy manner. He also announced that Catholics had a duty to protect the Holy Eucharist from profanation and to protect the faithful from scandal.

No less an authority than Cardinal Ratzinger was called upon to intervene. Then the head of the Congregation for the Doctrine of the Faith, Ratzinger sent a letter to the U.S. bishops' Task Force on Catholic Bishops and Catholic Politicians, headed by the now-disgraced Theodore McCarrick. His communication was meant for the bishops then at their annual meeting in Denver.

The future pope's memo was quite striking. He reiterated Church teaching that abortion and euthanasia are grave sins and that there is a grave and clear obligation to oppose them. He said it is never licit to obey or take part in a propaganda campaign in favor of such a law or to vote for it. When it comes to offering Communion to those who oppose Church teaching on abortion, the minister of Holy Communion may find himself in a situation where he *must* refuse to distribute it. A pastor must meet with an obstinate politician who persists in campaigning and voting for permissive abortion and euthanasia laws. The pastor should instruct him on the teachings of the Church and then warn him that he will be denied the Eucharist. He told the bishops that not all moral issues have the same moral weight as abortion and euthanasia. At the same time, he said Catholics could in good conscience be at odds with the Holy Father on questions of war and even capital punishment.

When it comes to voting, Ratzinger wrote that a Catholic was guilty of formal cooperation in evil and would be unworthy to receive Communion if he deliberately voted for a candidate because of the candidate's permissive stand on abortion or euthanasia. If the Catholic does not support the candidate's position on abortion, he may vote for him in the presence of "proportionate reasons." In reality, it is practically impossible to think of a proportionate reason that compares to millions of dead unborn babies.

In a shocking turn of Church politics, McCarrick refused to share Ratzinger's memo with the bishops and then proceeded to lie about it. McCarrick told them Ratzinger said withholding Communion was wholly up to the local bishop and nothing about pastors being required to withhold in certain circumstances. The bishops did not even know the full content of the memo until it was leaked to an Italian journalist some months later.

Ratzinger's memo, even after it leaked, did not settle the matter of voter guidance. In fact, voter guidance has been a political battle among members of the clergy for years. Unfortunately, Ratzinger is just one voice among many—though his voice is significantly more authoritative than those of his rivals.

We only need to consider one example from a leftist Catholic bishop to show the political pressures Catholics face from inside their own Church. Issued in February 2020, the document demonstrates how the Catholic Left is closely aligned with the policy preferences of the Democratic Party. Excluding abortion, it is a perfect example of the political preferences of the Left. And rhetorically, the Catholic Left tries to make the moral distinctions between different issues blurrier in order to allow politically liberal Catholics to choose other issues over abortion.

Published by Bishop Robert McElroy of San Diego, who is something of a darling of the Catholic Left, "Conscience, Candidates and Discipleship in Voting" is a paradigmatic example of how the Catholic Left operates. Instead of admitting that support for today's Democratic Party is support for abortion and an anti-Catholic agenda, McElroy equivocates between our moral duty to protect the unborn child and other considerations, including catastrophic man-made climate change and questions of character.

McElroy says Pope Francis "proposes starkly that our political lives must be seen as an essential element of our personal call to holiness." The pope, McElroy writes, "proposes that we can only fulfill our vocation as faithful citizens if we come to see in the very toxicity of our political culture at the current moment a call for deeper conversion to Jesus Christ." He says we must be missionaries of dialogue and civility in a moment that values neither. These slightly veiled barbs at Donald Trump and the Republican Party are hard to ignore and show where McElroy's allegiances lie.

While McElroy does cite aspects of "Catholic social teaching," including "the promotion of a culture and legal structures that protect the life of unborn children," the purpose of his voter guidance is to downplay the protection of the unborn. To do so, he turns to catastrophic man-made climate change. According to him, "there is a clear international scientific consensus that climate change caused by the use of fossil fuels and other human activities poses an existential threat to the very future of humanity." He says so-called climate change "threatens the future of humanity and particularly devastates the poor and the marginalized." This, as was discussed in a previous chapter, is an innovation on the part of McElroy and is included nowhere in Catholic social teaching; nor are many of the issues he tries to make more pressing in order to obfuscate our moral duty to fight abortion.

Putting abortion, which has taken 50 million lives or more in America, on the same moral plane as "catastrophic man-made climate change" is a significant abrogation of Catholic morality. He calls them "two monumental threats to human life." He says correctly, "the death toll from abortion is more immediate," but then says, "the long-term death toll from unchecked climate change is larger and threatens the very future of humanity." This is laughable and clearly motivated by an agenda identical to that of the Democratic Party.

He also puts abortion on the same plane as what he calls "the culture of exclusion." This culture of exclusion, he says, concerns not just "immigrants"—that is, illegal aliens—but also Muslims, Hispanics, and African Americans. He cites the "racist structures" of American politics that you're more likely to hear about in a grievance studies class than in Church teaching. Perhaps McElroy is not aware that under the Trump administration, blacks and Hispanics boasted the lowest unemployment figures in the history of our country. He also seems unaware of the massive governmental apparatus born of the 1964 Civil Rights Acts that puts the whole weight of the federal government, including the judiciary, into scouring out any vestige of racism, though not racism against whites through affirmative action in hiring and quotas in college admissions. He also leaves out the fact that the suicide rate for white men is skyrocketing, as is the incidence of drug addiction among whites and other pathologies among those who do not have such governmental protection.

I use McElroy's document because it voices the common complaints of the Left about the United States in general and Donald Trump in particular. It could have been a document written by any number of American or foreign bishops. It could have been written by Bishop Tobin of Newark or Cupich of Chicago, both favored by the current lineup in the Vatican. But the central point is that it is little different from the garden-variety leftism you're bound to find on college campuses, where young students are indoctrinated in anti-Catholic morality. The fact that some bishops have drunk from that poisoned chalice is a cause for concern.

Meanwhile, the unfavored bishops such as Cardinal Burke have spoken out in defense of those who oppose massive waves of Syrian refugees in Europe and who argue unashamedly that abortion alone is the preeminent issue of our time because of its horrific body count. Without a doubt, if we were killing almost a million refugees a year, the Catholic Left would roust itself to argue that that was the preeminent issue of our time. As it is, we are only talking about defenseless unborn babies.

Today, abortion is still the most pressing issue facing the Catholic voter. Fighting abortion, one of the gravest injustices known to man, is the most important priority for Catholics. According to Catholic teaching, defending the innocent is the bedrock of Catholic morality. Other issues may be worked towards—after all, we can work on more than one thing at a time—but abortion remains the most crucial.

With regard to the other issues, we may differ prudentially about how to address them, but we can never accept intrinsically evil policies, let alone collaborate in them. We must start with abortion, as the other problems, though serious, do not bear the same weight as the ongoing genocide of the unborn.

The fact that voter guidance is such a contentious issue only makes matters more difficult for Catholics. In addition to the political winds of the American system, we also have to pay attention to the trends among the clergy. In November 2019, the American bishops met to revise the voter guidance document and there was a donnybrook about where to place abortion. Chicago cardinal Blase

Cupich, who is very close to Pope Francis, said abortion is not the most important issue. He proposed, "Equally sacred, however, are the lives of the poor, those already born, the destitute, the abandoned and underprivileged, the vulnerable infirm and elderly exposed to covert euthanasia, the victims of human trafficking, new forms of slavery, and every form of rejection." This paragraph from the pope's *Gaudete et Exsultate* went down to defeat 143–69.

It was further decided that catastrophic man-man climate change is an important issue but not urgent and that in a narrow vote abortion would remain the preeminent issue. There was much hand-wringing and parsing to determine what "preeminent" means. And then to confuse matters further, a few months later the bishops released a series of videos to further help the Catholic voter and none was about abortion. See, political ping-pong.

One hot-button issue that goes wholly missing in the consideration of the bishops is the issue they probably hear the most in confession each week, consumption of pornography. It is mentioned only three times in this lengthy document. As far as I know, only two American bishops have written letters about it. There is little doubt that a significant portion of their parishioners view porn of the most vile and violent kind on a regular basis. To be sure, I am not aware of anything any of the presidential candidates intends to do about it. There is pressure on the right for President Trump's Domestic Policy Council to issue a document coming out against pornography and to declare it, as a few states already have, a public health crisis. There is also pressure on the

Department of Justice to begin prosecutions of "obscenity," which remains prosecutable under federal law. But there has been nothing concrete so far, and sadly little recognition of the problem from the bishops.

It should also be pointed out that the bishops' views on political issues have been harmed over the years not just by the way they handled the priest sex scandal, but by their intrusion into so many issues, many of which are not their competence. Many of the documents produced by the USCCB are not actually written by the bishops but by lay staff who, over the years, have had a decided leftward tilt, further harming the credibility of the bishops.

These controversies only generate confusion about what constitutes Catholic social teaching. And this is just within a single country. When it comes to comparing different nations to one another, it gets even hairier. Bishop Marcelo Sanchez Sorondo, chancellor of the Pontifical Academy of Social Sciences, quite infamously said that the Chinese Communist state was "extraordinary" and that "right now, those who are best implementing the social doctrine of the Church are the Chinese." What is a practicing Catholic supposed to make of that?

Here is one of the pope's closest advisers arguing from Catholic social teaching that a country that has militarized its population, forced abortion upon women, driven faithful Catholics underground, enslaved and imprisoned its opponents, and is even said to kill prisoners for their internal organs more closely lives Catholic social teaching than any other country in the world. This is both preposterous and scandalous.

Bishop Sanchez Sorondo said, "What people don't realize is that the central value in China is work, work, work. There's no other way, fundamentally it is like St. Paul said: he who doesn't work, doesn't eat." Presumably, Sanchez Sorondo knows about the widespread use of slave labor in China. He presumably knows how factories so overwork their employees that suicide among them is rampant.

So, Catholics may be rightly confused about to what extent Catholic social teaching should guide their political decision-making. The problem with Catholic social teaching is that it provides a general framework to think about things without ironing out specifics. What does it teach us about the minimum wage, for instance? If you ask politically leftist Catholics, the answer would be "more." The answer is always "more," "higher." If the minimum wage is $8.00, Catholic social teaching says it has to be $9.00, and then $10.00, and then $15.00. If you disagree with that, to the Catholic Left you are a bad Catholic, a cafeteria Catholic. But Catholic social teaching does not give a number for the minimum wage. It presumes we can work it out among ourselves. Catholic social teaching is not an oracle.

In the current day, why can't one infer that the "preferential option for the poor" in Catholic social teaching calls us to eliminate the corporate tax rate? Eliminate the death tax? Eliminate the Occupational Safety and Health Administration and the U.S. Department of Education? Each of these can be interpreted as harming the poor. Yet politically leftist Catholics would charge violations of Church teaching if we did. But who is right? Whose policy prescriptions fit best within Catholic social teaching?

Confusion regarding the role of Catholic social teaching is not necessarily a bad thing. It just means that there is no body of propositions that determines our political decision-making as Catholics. To suggest that certain propositions in politics or economics are magisterially taught is to confuse the faithful and even scandalize our separated brethren. Are we required to believe in catastrophic man-made climate change? Some say that we are and that even to question it is to place oneself outside the Church as a dissenter, a cafeteria Catholic. One often reads such silly things in left-wing Catholic punditry.

So while it may be an error in policy to suggest the answer is always more and more and more, it's also a mistake to invoke Catholic social teaching to support every concrete policy preference. As a result of this misuse of Church teaching, politically conservative Catholic voters may rightly be suspicious of lefty Catholics who come bearing Catholic social teaching. We are allowed as Catholics to use prudence to determine for ourselves how to apply Church social teaching. A preferential option for the poor? Fine. Lower corporate taxes so he can get a job. Close the border to illegal aliens so his wages will not suffer. These are legitimate solutions using Catholic social teaching, though they fall outside the policy prescriptions of the Democratic Party and even what some bishops will say.

Without a doubt, you already will have heard that Donald Trump has violated Catholic social teaching by reducing taxes, opening up the various oil pipelines, pulling out of the Paris Climate Accord, and reducing the budget for the Department of Education. But truth be told, Donald Trump is protecting Catholics from a Democratic Party that wants to destroy their ability to practice their faith. The party is fully aligned with the radical woke Left, with cancel culture, with masked men and women on the streets attacking those with whom they disagree. MAGA hat–wearing adults and kids are attacked by leftists on the streets of America. Your average Democrat in Washington, D.C., supports forcing girls to play sports with gender-confused boys. Targeting corruption in government and on Wall Street is a lower priority than forcing Christian bakers to prepare cakes for gay weddings and throttling Catholic nuns who do not want to pay for contraception and abortion. Regardless of what the Catholic Left may say, the Democrats are more concerned with rooting out traditional ways of life than they are with any economic agenda.

And the Democratic Party is only becoming more radical on the question of abortion. This is no longer the party of "safe, legal, and rare" abortion. Of course, that was always a lie. The

Clintons never met an abortion they didn't support. But even that slogan is now gone from the Democratic repertoire. Now Democratically controlled state legislatures are passing bills protecting the "right" to kill unborn babies up until the moment of birth. If *Roe* is overturned, these will remain law in these states, including New York and the formerly largely conservative Commonwealth of Virginia.

Transgenderism has now become a human right, even according to the supposed centrist Joe Biden. Biden doesn't just pay lip service to the transgender issue; he goes further than that. He calls it the most pressing human rights issue of our time. How could any practicing Catholic stomach support for cutting off healthy penises and breasts, especially of teens? That's what lefty Catholics like Joe Biden want you to vote for.

The Catholic vote will be essential to staving off the menace of the woke Left. Democrats will try every dirty trick to get Catholics to abandon Trump because they know that Catholics in the Rust Belt are essential to Trump's electoral coalition. But it's important that we stay the course and look at what's at stake. Democrats, regardless of whether they're led by nominal Catholics such as Joe Biden or cosmopolitan atheists, are dedicated to a social agenda that has declared war against the Catholic Church. President Trump, meanwhile, has done more to advance issues we are morally obliged to promote than any other president in recent memory. He has not only fought abortion and gender ideology, he has made it easier to practice our faith in these United States.

The choice is simple: Catholics must support Donald Trump's re-election bid.

Index